BEGINNERS GUIDE TO

WRITING YOUR LIFE STORY

BEGINNERS GUIDE TO

WRITING YOUR LIFE STORY

Leave a living legacy for family and friends

Graham L. Ascough

Published by:

Bas Publishing
ABN 30 106 181 542
F16/171 Collins Street
Melbourne Vic. 3000
Tel: (03) 9650 3200
Fax: (03) 9650 5077
Web: www.baspublishing.com.au
Email: mail@baspublishing.com.au

The National Library of Australia Cataloguing-in-Publication entry

Ascough, Graham L.
   Beginners guide to writing your life story : leave a living
   legacy for family and friends.

   ISBN 1 920910 70 0.

   1. Autobiography - Authorship. I. Title.

808.06692

Design & Layout: Ben Graham

DEDICATION

This is dedicated to Florence Edith Lawrence
A life long friend and mentor

Acknowledgements

I would like to pay a tribute to those who have helped to make this book a reality.

Rona Myers – For her positive enthusiasm and patience in typing this manuscript.

Rae Allen – For her professional input in structuring the material.

Valmai Gibson & Olive Laing – For all your help with grammatical construction.

Gael Hammer – My professional editor who was able to turn round much confused thinking to make it readable.

BAS Publishing – Especially Sam Basile and Ben Graham for their professional approach to this book.

Alan Hale – For his help in preparing a marketing strategy.

TEN TIPS FOR WRITING YOUR LIFE STORY

1. **Write with a sense of positive expectancy**

   Believe you have a story worth telling and leave a legacy for family and friends.

2. **Awaken the writer within**

   Begin now! You may be surprised to find what talent you have for this task.

3. **Write to communicate not to impress**

   Tell people about what you think and feel and not just what you have accomplished.

4. **You don't have to be perfect**

   Writing gives you the freedom to express yourself. Do not compare yourself with anyone else.

5. **Write with your head and heart - it has to be believable and entertaining**

   Live the moment you are writing about as you convey your thoughts to the page. Capture the mood. Readers will feel that what you are sharing is important to you.

6. **Write with honesty - elements of conflict, humour and pathos**

   Tell your story as it was, not how you would have liked it to be. Reveal yourself. Let people see the various aspects of you the person.

7. **Writing is simply speaking on paper**

   Writing as you speak is like engaging in a one on one conversation. Be chatty and choose words from your own vocabulary.

8. **Writing is hard work**

   Nothing of a worthwhile nature is achieved without a lot of effort, perseverance and resolve.

9. **Write at your own pace**

   Make it a pleasurable hobby not a chore. Be disciplined in setting aside time, but do not allow the project to dominate your life. Set your goals about how much and when to write, and review these regularly if necessary.

10. **Writing is a way of reviewing your life**

    Take time out for yourself as you review your life. You might not think that you have led a terribly interesting life, but the chances are, once you start writing it all down you will be surprised by how eventful it has been.

Contents

About The Author

Graham Ascough has a passion for writing, and a passion for people and their stories. Born at the beginning of the Great Depression he learned the need to be resourceful and resilient. He had the good fortune early in his career to be guided and encouraged by his employers. Even the manager of the Queensland Egg Board who sacked him after only one month for throwing rotten eggs at another office boy.

His career spans advertising, journalism, publishing, pastoral ministry and counselling. Thirty years ago, he started the North Shore Counselling & Personal Growth Centre in Sydney and was the first minister of religion in New South Wales to make the transition from pastoral ministry into full time counselling.

Concerned about seniors' issues and the effect of retirement on people he wrote the book *Oh Happy, Happy Days - New Rules of Retirement* which was published in 2002 by Crown Content, Melbourne. The book focuses on the emotional and psychological preparation for retirement.

After closing the counselling centre and "semi-retiring", Graham, together with his second wife Carmel, ran a bed & breakfast at Hunters Hill for five years. This was to be a transitional phase of retirement, but also proved to be an enriching experience.

In his seventy seven years in both his personal and working life he has been inspired, challenged, surprised and touched by the thousands of people with whom he has been in contact. He has been witness to their triumphs and failures, heard their darkest fears, their dreams, their goals. He has seen their strength and weakness in times of immense pain and struggle, and their joy and happiness in overcoming their difficulties, both real and imagined.

He was encouraged to write his own life story, and through the struggles and insecurities he experienced during this time, he was motivated to write this *Beginner's Guide to Writing Your Life Story*. He writes from personal experience in a way to help others to realise their potential and to make writing their life story interesting and entertaining.

Graham firmly believes men and women from all walks of life have one thing in common; they each have unique, rich life experiences that should be preserved for future generations. Writing their story can be one of the most important things they ever do; a living record that can be enjoyed by countless generations to come, and a permanent social history of our advancing country. We need to value our rich heritage.

It is his hope that this step-by-step guide will especially inspire the first time writer.

How To Use This Do-It-Yourself Manual

Writing your life story gives you the opportunity to explore, express and experience your life in all of its aspects. This book is a step-by-step guide for the inexperienced writer. We live by stories; now is the time to let your story unfold. Listen, trust yourself and follow your instinct. Let the person who lives deep within you come through as you write freely.

Write from the heart and probe subjects and feelings that affect you deeply. Know that you are not alone on this journey. Your shared struggles, fears and triumphs are the very soul of the art and craft of writing. Most of the examples used in this book are taken from Graham Ascough's life story called *Life is for Living*. The book is available from the author.

Some people need a writing schedule that works for them; others work at their own pace. There are no time limits to complete your story. Discipline and consistency in writing produce the best results.

Preparation For Writing Your Life Story

Lessons No. 1 to 5: Resist the temptation to start writing until you have finished Lesson 5. See yourself as a generator waiting to be switched on. Once you are turned on you will generate ideas as your batteries are fully charged and ready to go. At the beginning of Lesson 2 we suggest you make a list of events and experiences you would use in your rough draft. Lesson 3 will encourage you to experiment with different approaches to writing your life story. Lesson 4 concentrates on oral history taking for the person writing someone else's life story. Then with Lesson 5 produce your first rough draft.

Writing Your Life Story

Lessons No. 6 to 13: You are now ready to commence writing your life story chapter by chapter. Chapters 8-10 encourage you to develop your style and voice, connect with the reader and take your story to a deeper level. Chapter 11 offers guidance for when you feel blocked and cannot write. By Chapter 12 you will be ready to have your manuscript edited and the final chapter presents publishing suggestions.

Thought Starters

These will be found only in Lessons 1-3 to help you focus your thoughts during your preparation and research.

Your Jottings Journal

A notebook, or loose-leaf binder with tabs - here you record thoughts, ideas and memories as you research your story. It will become a valuable resource once you begin writing. Always have it at hand for you never know when inspiration will strike - even when you are dealing with something entirely unrelated.

Personal Preparation For Writing Your Life Story

"Many people live and die with their music still unplayed. They never dare to try."

— Mary Kay Ash

Everyone Has a Story Worth Telling

Each of us has a story worth telling. It does not matter what sort of life you have lived, the challenges and experiences you have faced have made you the person you are today. You might not think that you have led a terribly interesting life, but chances are, once you start writing it all down you will be surprised by how eventful it has been. The events do not have to be spectacular, the ordinary everyday life challenges can make interesting reading.

Life Is a Journey From Birth to Death

From the day we are born to the day we die, our life is a personal journey with many twists and turns, peaks and valleys, monotonous and adventurous experiences. Think about roads taken and not taken and the consequences that followed these decisions. Reflect on meaningful experiences, particularly the ones that have made a significant impact on your life.

Leaving A Living Legacy

One of the greatest gifts we can give to our family and friends is a creative legacy of stories that have inspired, challenged, surprised and touched us during our lifetime. Friends and family can share our triumphs and our failures and discern what life was like and what was important to us.

Do Not Let Your History Die With You

You have a vast amount of knowledge and experience to pass on to others. Life has taught you a lot about coping with the disappointments and the highlights of success. Your stories are valuable treasures for your family and community. It can be fascinating to reflect on special periods in your life, the events of our nation and people around you.

Your written history helps others to identify with you and trigger memories of their own life. Readers can go back from time to time and relive your exploits. Through the printed page your history is a wonderful means for others to remember, learn from you and gain insights into their own lives.

Example

In his widely acclaimed autobiography *A Fortunate Life*, A.B. Facey gives a candid, heartfelt and straightforward account of the many hardships he endured throughout his life. He went out to work at the age of eight at the beginning of last century in Western Australia. A veteran of the Gallipoli campaign he later became a farmer, but was forced off the land during the Great Depression. He joined the tramways and was active in the Tramways Union.

Summary: This is the story of an ordinary Australian who with no formal education successfully wrote a transparent examination of his life and person. The reader becomes engrossed in the story as he relives his life. He showed that despite great suffering and hardship he always retained his optimism and dignity and believed he had "a fortunate life". No one can read his story and not be inspired. Think what the world would have lost if he had not written his story.

Stories R Us

Bedtime stories stirred our imagination and became a part of our nightly ritual long before we started to read as children. As adults we love adventure stories, murder mysteries, true romance, science fiction and biographies. Stories are a way to escape into another world. There is a storyteller in each of us; some are simply more developed than others.

Sharing Life's Experiences

Each person's story is sacred and unique to the individual. You are who you are from your experiences of life. Sharing your story is only limited by a lack of confidence. The key to writing your life story is to believe you have something to say. Your story is your identity.

Writers Are Like Explorers

A life-story writer is like an explorer. An explorer has a purpose or objective. Your objective is to explore experiences and aspects of your life and share them with your readers.

The Best Person To Write Your Life Story

Ask yourself the question "Who else would be prepared to write my life story?" Usually the response would be "No one but me". Don't wait around. Tackle it before it is too late. You may be surprised to find what talent you have for this task.

Do Not Postpone Writing Your Life Story

In a busy world it can be difficult to find the time and who really knows when it is the perfect time to commence writing your life story. If you want to write your life story do something about it now. Some people are "gonna people" – always "gonna" do something but never get around to doing it. They miss so many opportunities by procrastination. Tell friends what you are doing. This helps you to stay committed to your project.

Memories

Some would say that they cannot remember events from long ago and believe them to be lost for good. But they are simply buried deep within your subconscious. Through exercises such as relaxing, meditating and writing exercises, you will be able to access the storehouse of the mind and be amazed at what you remember.

Selective Memory

We do not know why we remember some pivotal experiences and forget others. It could be that these are the ones we are prepared to face at this time. Have the courage to show your struggles, disappointments and the mistakes you have made. Write in a way that is positive, sharing what you have learned from each experience. Do not be bogged down with regrets.

Be Self-Motivated

You need to be self-motivated. There may be no one to encourage you, so you need to be focused on the task at hand. To be self-motivated you need to be excited by the project.

Do not let limitations like busyness, shyness, reserve or even lack of exact knowledge of written English expression hold you back. All of these can be overcome providing writing your life story has become a high priority.

Let Readers See The Real You

Many go through life playing games and covering up their real feelings. Perhaps this is the first opportunity you have to be authentic. Reach deep down and share your fears, anxieties and successes. Let people see the various aspects of your character.

If you write with truth and integrity, people could discover a new dimension to your character. Tell your story as it is and do not attempt to cover up your mistakes or justify your actions as you chose the various paths in your journey.

Writing For Family and Friends

Bear in mind your main reason for writing your life story. For some it is a way to share discoveries made about life. You may even feel you are the carrier of a message that could be helpful to others. Others may see it as a way to touch their audience in a manner that has not been possible before.

Your main group of readers will probably be your family and friends. They know you, or at least think they do. Some of their previously held views of you will no doubt be challenged as they read your story. Even if we have very close relationships with our family and friends we do not always tell them everything we feel and think. As you write you might still decide not to *tell all*, but you may surprise them with some revelations. Keep in mind most life storywriters will never be the "movers and shakers" of the world or big business, just ordinary people wishing to share their journey.

Do Not Apologise

When you commence to write your story make a simple statement that this is all about you and your history. Do not apologise for using the personal pronoun "I" and making "I" statements. Tell your story your way and write in a positive and enriching manner.

Take A Wide Angled View Of Life

Life has many facets and phases and we need to take a wide angled view of them all. As you focus on different aspects of your life look for specific details. You need not cover every phase of your life or each experience in the same way. Be selective. Some may compel you to delve deeper, but at other times you will just skim over material that you feel is not so important.

Write With Honesty

Do not hide yourself from view by talking about events while revealing little about you the person. This is not fair to the reader or yourself. Tell people about what you think and feel and have accomplished. It need not be bragging. It is a time for honesty, openness and letting as much as you feel possible to come through your writing.

Age Is A Writing Asset – Not A Liability

A question asked regularly is: "Am I too old for the task or is it too big a job for me to tackle?" Age is an asset for the life storywriter as there is a vast range of knowledge and experiences. Once you tackle this project it will surprise you what you can achieve. The project can be more manageable by writing a number of essays on different aspects of your life e.g. school days, the land I once knew, relationships, fears, health concerns, work, sporting and religious activities.

Make An Investment of Time and Energy

We make many kinds of investments such as marriage, property, stocks and shares, work, life and much more. See writing your life story as a wise investment, far better than watching television. See the time put towards this as time well spent. It is a venture with added benefits.

Stimulate Your Brain

Writing your life story can be an inspiring and encouraging project. See it as a hobby that stimulates your mind and brain. Maybe even a safeguard against dementia. It is a way for you to use leisure moments in a productive manner. Life is too short to be serious all the time. Each joyful and sad moment has its own intensity and needs to be expressed with feeling. Some people may find it easier to write about sad moments as they seem to linger longer than the joyful events.

If you are happy, make it obvious to your reader by paying attention to the small experiences of life which have a way to help define who you are by the way you reacted. If what you are sharing brings sadness, let it flow through your words. Your story can flow from joy to sadness, exhilaration to emptiness in a few short, crisp sentences.

Example

As a young minister at West Pennant Hills I was keen to win souls, I was very critical and judgmental. In my pious belief I resolved never to go to a wedding reception where liquor was served. I had forgotten the story of the wedding in Cana where Christ was present and performed the miracle of turning water into wine.

The parents of the bride who loved and respected me and wanted me to attend the reception challenged me. They listened to my reasoning and then told me in no uncertain words what they felt about my sanctimonious attitude. Listening to their logical and rational argument I reconsidered my decision and attended the reception and enjoyed the experience very much. I had to learn that everything in moderation is acceptable. Today I drink socially and have been known to be a little merry on a couple of occasions.

Summary: This story is to make the reader think. I start off being self-righteous and hook the reader in by my attitude. Openness and honesty follow as I am challenged and my personal boundaries extended. There is a surprise factor when drinking gets a little out of hand. The reader gains new insights about the main character of the story. This is a good illustration of changing values.

Identifying Your Writing Purpose

When writing your life story keep your purpose clearly in mind, for whatever your motivation, it will help you with self-expression. Some people feel they have been misunderstood all their life and wish to set the record straight. Others write because they feel they have something worthwhile to say to help others along the way. There are also people who believe they are born storytellers and find writing a means of creative expression.

Make Writing A Pleasurable Experience

You could be struggling with conflicts and searching for answers - writing your life story becomes a part of this search. Make the process of writing a pleasurable experience. Do not put too many demands on yourself by trying to achieve perfection. Be disciplined in setting aside time, but do not allow the project to dominate your life.

Laugh and cry along the way. Relive the fun experiences you recall.

The Effect Of Your Book On Self and Others

Writing your life story could well have a major effect on you. As you review your life with its successes and failures you will no doubt conclude that you have accomplished much. The successes may not warrant a headline in the newspaper or a medal or diploma, but I hope you will realise that you have influenced many lives. No one knows exactly what the impact of your writing will have on others. Books have a way of travelling far and wide and of being read by people you do not know. The hard work involved is worth all the effort even if it has only had a positive influence on one person.

Do not compare your autobiography with others. Let it stand alone and be judged by the readers according to the way it affected them. Be committed to getting your inner truth down on paper.

THOUGHT STARTERS FOR LESSON ONE

1. Think of the words of William Saroyan "If you practice an art faithfully it will make you wise". What benefits do you think you will receive by writing your life story?

2. What do you believe is the main message you wish to convey?

3. Are you prepared to put time and effort into this project? It could be difficult and frustrating as well as rewarding.

4. Are you willing to be open through self-disclosure?

5. Every life is precious and yours is no exception. Ordinary events in your life can appear to be extraordinary from another person's perspective.

WRITING EXERCISES FOR LESSON ONE

1. What writers do is write. The material you write in your Jottings Journal may be basic material you will use in writing your life story.

   Write 300 words on one of the following:

   (i) A holiday that stands out in your memory.

        OR

   (ii) A childhood experience that you remember clearly.

        OR

   (iii) Describe three close friends – write 100 words for each friend.

2. Now write on the same subject and cut down the story to 200 words.

3. Compare both stories

    (i)   Compare the content of both stories.

    (ii)   Study story momentum.

Getting Started – Basic Guidelines For Beginners

*"Writers come from persons who
have a story to tell"*

— Fulton Oursler

Where To Write - The Writer's Den

Find a spot in your home where you will be comfortable, where you can explore your inner thoughts, where you can be inspired. Some writers like music in the background as they write; others need complete silence and solitude for thoughts to surface. Create an atmosphere that is conducive to good writing. Be sure there is sufficient space, light, warmth/coolness. Have all that you might need in the way of pens, notebooks, some kind of filing system, a tape recorder perhaps and even paperclips at hand.

What To Write With - Be Comfortable With Your Writing Tools

In our world of modern technology, the computer has become a popular and convenient tool. With built-in spell and grammar checks and its thesaurus, the word processor allows us to save, edit and move text around easily. Other writers might lack the availability of a computer and use a typewriter, or simply prefer to use a pen.

Whatever method you use to record your story it is essential that you always backup your material. Take a copy of completed work even if writing longhand or using a manual typewriter. You just never know when something might happen to the original. It would be frustrating to have to rewrite pages of work if your computer system failed or if your pet took a liking to your story and decided to have a meal of it.

Physical disabilities need not stop anyone from writing. It is just a matter of exploring different ways of getting your story down on paper. Professional help is available through the Department of Ageing and Disability in each capital city. Local community centres might also have people available to assist. Your story can also be recorded by a friend or family member. We look at this more thoroughly in Lesson Four.

When to Write - Devise Your Own Writing Plan

No two individuals are the same so take time to decide when you are most likely to be free from interruptions such as telephone, family and household chores; when you are likely to be at your most productive. Some people are early birds and feel they do their best work in the morning for they feel fresh in mind and thought and able to write freely. Setting a regular time of day is important, for if there is no planned approach you may meander along and end up nowhere, except perhaps very frustrated. It may be necessary to ask other members of the household not to interrupt you during your chosen time.

Discipline yourself to meet your commitment. Don't give up if the going gets tough, but take a break from your writing and do something entirely different such as going for a walk, to a movie, etc. Nothing of a worthwhile nature is achieved without a lot of effort, perseverance and resolve.

Consistency Improves Your Writing Style

The sporting champions you watch at a major sporting event get there through training, persistence and determination. The more time they spend in training the better they get. The same is true about the consistency in writing. With experience you will feel more confident in what you have to say. Words will flow more freely. You do not have to write at length to reveal your scholarly ability, just be natural, simple and direct.

How Much To Write

Some writers decide they will spend (x) number of hours per day on their project. Others follow the formula of writing so many pages per day. Perhaps break up your story writing into small parcels. When you decide what format your story will take, such as memoirs, a series of essays, a chapter for different time periods or events in your life, you will have a better idea of how much time or how many pages to commit to per session.

Live The Moment

Live the moment you are writing about as you convey your thoughts to the page. Capture the mood. Readers will feel that what you are sharing is important to you. Do not try to control these moments, simply go with them and see what happens.

Where To Record Information - Using The "Jottings Journal"

The Jottings Journal is a valuable tool as you write your life story. It can simply be a loose-leaf notebook where you record information as you collect it; memories of people, dates, time, events, experiences and observations from life, and your ideas for telling your story. It is a place where you can be honest with yourself as you look at how events or people influenced you or have affected your life in some way. In such a project, thoughts and ideas are easily lost if not recorded straight away. Always have a notepad and pen with you wherever you are - you never know when inspiration will strike. This will be a great source of encouragement and help as you begin your writing.

Research - Where to begin?

Some people might be happy just to write about what they remember without delving too deep. For those who wish for a more detailed study there are many sources of information. Start in your home. Simply walking around your home, garden or neighbourhood can generate memories long forgotten. Go through your photographs, old letters, school report cards, work papers, certificates, music, clothing, ornaments or toys. Many ordinary things will help you recall memories. Be sure to have your notebook with you as you do this, you never know when something will trigger a thought.

Go to the library and look up old newspapers. Read what world and local events happened at the time of your birth and during your lifetime. Reflect on who or what has influenced you.

Unlocking Memories – Sensory Triggers

In a way, exploring your memories is like retrieving information from a computer database (or an old library card catalogue, if you are not computer literate). But we usually need some kind of key to gain access and, in the case of our memory, that key or trigger might come from one of the senses. Smell is one of our strongest senses and can be very powerful in retrieving past events and experiences. For example the brief whiff of a perfume, a stable odour, the scent of a flower can take you back to a person or experience. A song lyric or melody, a colour, the feel of a particular fabric or the taste of a favourite food can all trigger personal memory.

Make a list of your triggers. Work through each of the senses: sight, sound, smell, touch, taste. It might be helpful to put yourself in actual contact with one or more of the triggers on your list. For example, pieces of fabric, a balloon, play a piece of music, or whatever might be your trigger. For each sense, jot down in just a few words anything that seems to bring out an emotional response. As you make your lists, put a mark by any item on the list that jumps out at you as being particularly powerful. Don't worry yet about precisely what makes it so potent; you can look at that in more detail later.

Once you have your list take your time and focus on one trigger at a time. Start with the items you marked when you were making the lists. Record everything this exercise produces. Once you've got a clear mental image of the thing, try to identify any other images or emotions that seem to be related. Let your mind explore whatever associated images come to mind.

Free Writing As A Means of Unlocking Memories

Free writing is spontaneous writing for a set period of time. Choose a moment you don't remember well, perhaps an embarrassing moment, your first kiss or your first day at school. Set a timer, five minutes is good for a start, and write down all that comes to mind. Do not stop writing during the full amount of time. If you get stuck just write anything that comes to mind, even if it does not make sense. Don't plan or think about what you are writing, just let your pen do the work as quickly as you can. Some of the writing will not be useful. However it is possible you will come up with ideas and phrases that lead you in a new direction and can result in the discovery of some other memory or insight. This is a valuable tool that can be used at any time during your project.

Photographs Are A Valuable Source of Memories

Photographs hold memories of the past and are a great source of information. When looking at photos ask yourself some relevant questions. Here are a few as a guide:

> Where was this taken?
>
> What was the occasion?
>
> What was I wearing?
>
> Who else was in the photo?
>
> What were my feelings towards other people in the shot?
>
> Why was I happy, sad, or surprised?

Treasured Mementos

Everyone has some kind of treasure box containing little gems of their past. What happened to the ribbon you won for coming first? Where is the little ball of saved string? Where did that dried flower come from that fell out of your book? What made you keep that theatre programme? What is the significance of that broken button? Whose lock of hair is that? Many and varied items that to others may be rubbish were important enough to you to be tucked away - things you have never wanted to discard.

Pick up each item. Allow yourself to become immersed in its energy.

What emotion or memory does it trigger first as you pick it up?

Where did it come from?

What were you doing at the time?

Where were you?

Who else was involved?

How do you feel about those around you?

What was happening in the world?

Start recording what you are experiencing. And like before, once you have a clear mental image of where the item is from, try to identify any other images or emotions that seem to be related.

The House That Jack Built – Rooms of Memories

Take a walk through the house you lived in as a child, or your grandmother's house, or maybe the first house you bought as an adult. Take out a large piece of paper and actually draw a plan of it. You are at the front door. Are there steps leading to it, or is it on level ground? What is ahead of you, a hall, or does it lead straight into a room? Continue drawing the rooms – the bathrooms, bedrooms, kitchen and living rooms. Now furnish the rooms. Where was the furniture? What colour was the carpet, linoleum, or bare floors? What pictures were on the wall? Include as much detail as you can of the house, and surrounding yard and beyond if you wish. Describe things of the time that perhaps are not in common use today e.g. the ice chest, meat safe, copper, wringer, clothes props, large radios, bakelite telephones etc.

Put yourself in the room and allow your writing to take you back to that place. Explore your thoughts about the place and its surroundings. Consider the age you were when you lived there and the people around you.

At the end of this lesson you will find a research checklist to help you review your life.

Research – Interviewing Friends And Family

Another great source of research for writing is to reminisce with family or friends. Having a chat with elderly relatives can provide you with a lot of background information. Talk to siblings, old family friends, anyone who you feel might be able to add to your knowledge, particularly of your earlier days, or important people in your life.

Bear in mind though we tend to remember things differently. A classic example: five people witness an accident yet all five relate the accident differently in some way. This is because we each have our own individual way of interpreting what we see through our perspective. Another example is a sibling might say their parents never argued, but another might recall many fiery arguments. Sometimes it is simply a case of choosing what one wants to remember.

As you sift through information, you almost become a detective. Follow any leads and see where they take you. Some leads will be dead ends, while others will open up a new train of thought. Good note taking helps you to sift through conflicting thoughts and reach logical conclusions. In the end though, you are writing your story from your viewpoint.

Seven Interviewing Skills For Researchers

Although usually you would simply sit and chat (rather than a formal interview) with a relative or friend as you research your history, the following interviewing skills could be of value.

1. **Respect the interviewee's rights**

   The interviewee has the right to refuse to answer a question.

2. **Use simple, clearly worded questions**

   Be clear with the questions you want answered.

3. **Allow for silence**

   Let silence happen. Do not be in a hurry to jump in and "kill" the silence. Some valuable information could be forthcoming.

4. **Control the interview**

   Some people have a tendency to drift from the question being asked. Be in control.

5. **Check and recheck**

   Make sure that you clearly understand the information that has been disclosed.

6. **Confidentiality**

   Be sure to receive permission to quote your source if you use it in your story. Get permission in writing.

7. **Show your appreciation**

   Recognise the interviewee's contribution and show your appreciation for the time and effort. Be sensitive and do not take people for granted.

Ethics Of Interviewing

Be upfront with the people you interview, especially if you are going to feature them in your story. Sometimes it is wise to get written consent. Some may even ask to read what you write before it is published.

How To Process Research Material

1. **Access Information:** Collect as much information that you feel is necessary in your Jottings Journal.

2. **Analyse:** Take time to analyse the information to make sure that it is factual.

3. **Evaluate:** Decide what you will use in your writing by knowing why you want to write your life story.

4. **Format Chapters:** Start to see how the chapters will fall into place in your story. This is achieved by following a story structure that allows you to move from point to point. Remember things can be changed around at any time.

5. **Reflection:** Take time to reflect on your outline, chapter headings, story content, and the way the story sounds (voice) and how it moves along (pace).

6. **Action:** Nothing will happen unless you make it. You will be ready to commence writing your life story when you have processed your research material.

The process of information leads to further exploration. These are the keystones and not the finished product. Process gives your writing a way to flow and come together as you explore aspects from childhood to the present time.

Research Check List No. 1 – Review Your Life

Here are some topics that may help you as you prepare to write your life story. Record your thoughts as you progress through the list.

Parents: Background, personality, work ethic, strengths and weaknesses.

Siblings: Number of children in family. Where do you fit in? Your relationship to siblings, then and now.

Relatives: Uncles, aunts, grandparents, adopted uncles and aunts, cousins. Did you have favourites? Any that stood out?

Environment: Where did you live? Describe your home. What was your room like? Did you have your own room? Things you remember about your home.

Your Neighbourhood: Describe your neighbours, other families you shared with. Was it affluent or poor? Identities that stand out - playmates.

School Days: Where did you go to school? Any teachers who stand out? What kind of student were you? Did you excel at school and win prizes? Did you enjoy school? School uniform and games you played. How did you get to school?

Sport: Were you interested in sport? What did you play? Were you a good sport? Are you still interested in sport? Does it play an important part in your life?

Pets: Do you remember any special pets? What were they? What were their names? What happened to them?

Holidays: Are there any holidays that stand out from your childhood? Destinations you have visited – good or bad experiences. Places you would like to visit and why.

Spirituality: Do you see yourself as a spiritual person? As a child did you attend religious instruction? Do you believe in God?

Educational Achievement: Your attitude to education after leaving school. Which exams did you pass? Or diplomas did you receive? Your attitude to lifelong learning. Describe your skills.

Work: Did you find it difficult to decide what you wanted to do in life? Describe your working life. Were you happy? Career changes, bosses, people you remember.

Adolescence: Adventures. Did you travel overseas? Friendships. Describe this period.

Dating: Significant people in your life. Thoughts about love, romance, intimacy and sex.

Marriage: How did you meet your partner? Marriage highlights. Family. Responsibilities. Divorce. Re-marriage. Children/relationships.

Success/Failures: Things you were good at – work and home. Turning points in your life. Successes. Disappointments. Any regrets?

Significant Events: Events that have made an impact upon your life.

Significant People: People who have played an important part in your life – parents, friends, colleagues and workmates.

Roads Taken/Not Taken: Significant turning points in your life. Opportunities taken or missed.

Death: Death of spouse, child, parent, close friend – the effect upon your life.

Illness: Have you, or a member of your family or friends, suffered any severe illness? Have there been any disabilities? How has this affected you?

Special Moments: A discovery you made, an award or recognition you received, a conversation that was special; disappointments that deeply affected you, a time of solitude that offered insight.

Goals: What are you current goals – long term, short term?

Dreams: Do you have recurrent dreams? Do you pay attention to your dreams?

Being Single: Advantages/disadvantages. What is it like living in a world made for couples? How have you experienced loneliness, independence, holidays, networking?

Special Celebrations: Birthdays, Christmas, family reunions, difficult crises, tragedy, special recognition.

Research Check List No. 2 – Major Turning Points In Life's Journey

Make a list of crucial events that took place at this time in your life - births, deaths, marriages, adventures and milestones.

Prepare a list of friends and enemies. Note any special relationships.

List all the jobs you held.

Think of your educational training, also skills you acquired from life.

Don't forget historical events and trends that helped shape your life.

Think of games you played; sports you were involved in.

Share what you thought you would like to do when you grew up.

Hopes, dreams and goals, fears and anxieties.

These are only some suggestions to help stimulate thoughts and ideas.

Stop Researching and Start Writing

The question most commonly asked is "How do I know I have sufficient material?" The answer is simple - you will never have completed research - there is always more to explore. You just have to make the decision to start. You can resume research if you feel it is necessary when facts are not clear, or something you write triggers other memories.

THOUGHT STARTERS FOR LESSON TWO

1. A writer needs a balanced approach to life. Interaction with others, recreation and regular family and household activities provides a means for you to come back to your writing refreshed and ready to continue. Good to remember especially when you feel bogged down in your writing.

2. At this early stage of preparation push aside any negative thinking that writing your life story is too much like hard work. Stay motivated! Enjoy the process.

3. Recognise the importance of research and begin collecting old newspaper cuttings, photographs and other memorabilia which will give you story ideas.

WRITING EXERCISE FOR LESSON TWO

1. Write a story about a significant turning point in your life. Write about the feelings associated with the experience, the effect it had on you. This is an exercise in learning to write from the heart. Limit your story to 500 words.

2. Now write down in 100 words how you felt about this experience.

3. As preparation for writing your life story jot down in very rough form stories, events and experiences you would like to include. Do not write the story, use headings only.

Different Approaches To Writing Your Life Story

*"We are apprentices in a craft where
no one ever becomes a master."*

- Ernest Hemingway

Different Approaches Suit Different People

Different approaches suit different people. Some will have a preference for the chronological/narrative approach; others like to deal with significant experiences and write poems, memoirs or essays.

Think about yourself and the way you face life. Do you gather facts in a logical manner exploring alternatives as you go? Or do you work from the experiential level and make events in life a learning experience? Some people love to write letters or were good at essay writing when in school. Whatever approach you take, remember – be prepared to revise your structure if it does not seem to flow freely, and stay motivated.

Chronological/Narrative

This is the most common approach used to write a life story. It will flow in a sequential order starting with details of what the writer knows of immediate ancestors – parents and grandparents – and then the writer is introduced. Chronological approaches can vary in style, the most familiar being the time-line. Divide your life into segments, e.g. 0-10 years, 11-20 years etc. Discuss these periods while focussing on special events. This approach helps the reader to see how you remember yourself to be at a given time and how you responded.

Some chronological writers record their history up to the present in a factual form without much personal insight or explanation of reactions. Although this is the choice of the writer, it can make for boring reading.

Genealogical

Genealogical research is pursued with enthusiasm by many people. State and local libraries have facilities for family research and local history societies have much information to assist in this pursuit. Help can be found through the Society of Australian Genealogists and the Church of Jesus Christ and the Latter Day Saints have family history centres around the world. Other sources include church records, government departments - Births Deaths and Marriages, newspapers, wills, probate records and cemeteries. Old family bibles can also be of value. The Internet has made this practice much more accessible to the ordinary person.

Tracing one's family of origin can be a fascinating and revealing exercise. Some use this knowledge of their ancestors in their own life story. Information about immediate ancestry and historical periods may provide insights into housing, finances, religion, politics, child rearing etc. The weakness in using this approach is that the main character, you, could be lost in stories about other people. However, you could add diagrams and charts to help your reader perceive you more clearly through a better understanding of your family history.

When using the genealogical approach, older relatives are a good source of information. They have lived through many experiences and can relate to the life and times of that period. Their memory recall of those days can sometimes be more accurate than dealing with the present. However, as we get older we sometimes tend to "confabulate" - to combine memories into stories with an element of truth. Such memories are difficult to assess for accuracy, unlike more recent events. Many people regret that they did not take the time to ask parents and grandparents details of their lives earlier. Apart from their memories, they could well have had provided valuable research material such as letters, cards, photographs, films and newspaper clippings.

Writing Your Personal Memoirs

Memoirs are a collection of stories, a personal account of events of a particular period or series of events in one's life - for example, war service, career, parenthood etc. The list is endless. You might select between 10 and 20 of life's experiences and write about them. To have a balanced approach a memoir should contain a selection of experiences – good and bad.

Story Telling

In the story telling approach the creative writer builds the story around a theme, carefully weaving the facts as the story evolves. Emotional appeal is created through blending words and experiences with skilful handling of the facts.

Some people are great storytellers – some better than others. If you have a flair for creativity, curiosity and imagination you may find this approach worth trying. As the story evolves it is natural that people will read between the lines; as a relationship develops, there must be truthfulness that appeals to the intelligence of the reader at all times.

Poetry Writing

A poet is the spokesperson for expressions of the heart which can touch all areas of life. Poetry, like all life that is abundant and genuine, must be vivid and vital in expression. The poet speaks to the mind or the soul through the senses. People who think deeply may find this approach very successful. They may write a number of poems from different times in their lives and put them into booklet form as their life story.

Joint Venture Writing Project

A life story can be written as a joint venture by two or more people – perhaps by a couple or a family. If the joint venture project is that of a couple, the first chapter deals with life before they met. Each person then writes about the different aspects of their lives. When this is done the couple decide on a structure for presentation. There is no reason why the two accounts should not be placed after each other and bound in one book. Another way the joint venture project can be approached is by each person writing their own life story and placing them in the same volume together.

Letters To Family and Friends

A well written letter can hold your attention - from beginning to end - about events, recollections and perceptions. Good letter writers are quite gifted and often have a chatty style and a special knack that helps them relive a situation on paper and their excitement comes alive as the moment is being shared. A variation of this approach is called "Letters To My Children". It is another way of sharing significant experiences. A letter can be a bit more relaxed and chatty. There is not much difference between memoir, letter or essay writing.

Oral History Writers

You can have someone else write your life story, ideal if you have difficulty putting your thoughts down on paper. Or it could be that you intend writing the life story of a family member or friend. Oral history writers usually have extensive questionnaires to fill in to trigger memories of past events. They also use phone, tape or audio-visual interviews to gather information. On completion of their research, a rough draft is presented in a story structure before the final presentation. We cover this extensively in Lesson Four. The professional oral history writer may have contact with graphic artists and publishers who handle small print runs. If you chose this path be sure at the beginning to obtain a quote in writing for the completed work, including any publishing costs.

Creative – Art and Story

Some creative people bring their story alive by combining their art with words. This form of creative expression allows the writer to communicate in a very original way their thoughts on important experiences in their lives. The art form and writing style can be very thought provoking. Some creative writers use cartoons, quotes and drawings to stimulate attention.

Frame Your Photo With Words

"A picture is worth a thousand words" can be interpreted "a picture is worth writing a thousand words". This approach allows people great scope for combining different styles of presentation. Some life story writers gather photographs and write stories around them. Photographs are proof of our existence, of our place within our families, community and circle of friends. Look at each photo objectively and describe what you see. Who were they? What did they do? What were times like in those days? Even if it is hard for you to remember the circumstances surrounding the photo, use the clues you find to reconstruct the moment.

The Scrapbook

People use photographs to write about significant moments in their lives. The scrapbook is a slightly different approach. Many of us have at least one box of special items collected over time that we have been reluctant to throw out. Objects, like photographs, hold the memories from the past. These can include cuttings from newspapers, certificates, old travel tickets, medals, ribbons from events, a baby's shoe, pressed flowers, a lock of hair, photos and all manner of relics from the past. If you have a computer and scanner, you can scan these and print them into your story. Write an account or anecdote about each item. Share your emotions about them as you write.

Stories From Your Diary

Many people keep diaries or journals about life's experiences. Some do this daily, weekly or maybe just when experiencing special events. If you are a diary writer you can use this as a basis to write your life story. Tristine Rainer, author of *The New Diary* writes "A journal is a personal book in which creativity, play and self therapy interweave, foster and compliment each other... it can help you to understand your past, discover your present and create your future". It is a way of reconstructing your life and showing the direction you are taking. This information is valuable research material.

Faction Writing

This is a combination of fact and fiction. The writer focuses on fiction and includes disguised historical facts that hides the writer's personal identity and protects privacy. The difference between the faction writer and the storyteller is that the faction writer embellishes the story to hide the true identity of the character. The storyteller can embellish the story to produce colour and imagination that seeks to reveal the true identity of the character. The main emphasis is upon the fiction story and the intrigue that develops throughout hides what is fact or fiction. This is the writer's purpose.

Wisdom Writing

A person's way of life is based upon their personal philosophy – their viewpoint, beliefs and values. Knowing this helps the reader to see how a person thinks, what they value and how they respect themselves and others. Values and beliefs are revealed through actions and reactions. Their philosophy is discovered through reading the life story. What is good for one person is not always good for another, but we can understand a lot more about a person through their living environment, personality, educational achievements, age, health and other experiences expressed through their writing.

Decide The Best Approach For You

After reading the description of the various approaches to writing your life story, be prepared to experiment. Once you have decided on the method, go for it. Writing your life story is a way to discern your future as you look back on your life and start to see a pattern evolving.

Whatever approach you take, revisiting the past can be enjoyable and thought-provoking. The Swedish philosopher, Soren Kirkegard said: "To dare is to lose one's footing temporarily; to not dare is to lose one's life". Be one of the daring ones.

Summary of The Different Approaches to Writing Your Life Story

1. **Narrative/Chronological**

   If you are good at attention to detail and have a strong structural approach to life.

2. **Storyteller**

   If you see yourself as a teller of yarns.

3. **The memoir writer**

   You may have been good at writing essays at school. You could write a series of short story length essays or memoirs.

4. **The poet**

   If you feel that you are the sensitive, romantic or a spiritual type.

5. **Joint Venture**

   You may see yourself as an experimenter with life history writing. This is a combined approach e.g. husband and wife.

6. **Family historian**

   If you love tracing your family history, try the genealogical approach coupled with stories about ancestors.

7. **The letter writer**

   If you are able to write interesting descriptive letters, try the "Letters to my Family and Friends" approach.

8. **Oral historian**

   You want help from a professional writer who will actually write the story for you. Through a series of interviews and research, the writer puts the life story together and often sees it through to publication.

9. **Creative – art & story**

For the creative and imaginative (one page art, one page story).

10. **Photo-story**

Write stories about photographs.

11. **Scrap book**

You love craft and want to make a scrapbook of photographs, newspaper clippings and all manner of memorabilia.

12. **The diary writer**

If you love to write a diary - on a daily basis or on special occasions. This offers vast amount of historical information. However, some diaries are only for private expression, not public information.

13. **Faction writer**

Perhaps you are a shy or very private person who hates the limelight. Or, perhaps you want to write you life story but need to hide your identity. Try the novel, short story or "faction" (combination of fact and fiction) approach.

14. **The Wisdom writer**

If you are prepared to share your philosophy as you deal with your successes, failures and disappointments. For those who are prepared to share pearls of wisdom that have been helpful.

THOUGHT STARTERS FOR LESSON THREE

1. There are so many different approaches to writing your life story. The chronological/narrative, memoirs, stories from life and essays. These stories focus around special events.

2. As you reflect on your life do you see yourself as a teller of yarns? In this case you might see yourself as a storyteller.

3. You may be a good letter writer and people love your letters because they are interesting. You may decide to write a series of letters to family and friends. This could help them to know you even more intimately.

4. Perhaps you are involved in research of your family history. As the family tree starts to evolve you may discover some stories that fit into your writing.

5. No approach is set in concrete. If one approach does not work for you, try another

WRITING EXERCISES FOR LESSON THREE

1. In order to help you select a style that suits you try these different approaches:

   (a) Write a story from your childhood selecting the best approach that you feel suits you.

   (b) Try writing a poem about a childhood experience and see how it flows.

   (c) Experiment with a creative approach – "Letters to my Family and Friends", the scrap book.

2. Write 250 words in your Jottings Journal about the approach that best suits you and why.

Writing Someone Else's Story

"We are writers and we never ask one another where we get our ideas; we know we don't know."

- **Stephen King**

Some Cannot Write Their Own Story

For whatever reason, a parent or grandparent may not wish to write their life story, but are willing to share it orally with someone else who is prepared to collate the information and get it down on paper. For the purpose of this lesson I am suggesting the recorder may be a member of the family – son or daughter - but of course they need not be and all the material in this lesson can be adapted to suit the relationship of the recorder to the storyteller.

There are some professional oral history writers who offer this service for a fee. They record the information and present it in story form.

Why Collect Oral History?

So much is lost when an older person dies without leaving behind their experiences and memories. For instance, those in their 80s and 90s have lived the length of one of the most tumultuous centuries ever. The 20th century has been one of enormous change and advancement: technologically, culturally and socially. As longtime witnesses to this eventful era they could well have interesting stories to tell. I personally lament that I did not capture stories from my own parents or grandparents. Do not make the same mistake. Unless we preserve these memories and stories they will disappear forever. Historians have recognised that the everyday memories of everyday people, not just the rich and famous, have historical significance.

Convincing Parents/Grandparents /Relatives

If you wish to record your parent's history you may need to convince them they have a story worth telling. The same applies to a grandparent or other relative. For the purpose of this exercise I have focused on convincing the recorder's parent/s.

The suggestion to record their life story may come as a surprise to them so give them time to adjust to the idea before they give you an answer. Expect resistance but help them to overcome their shyness and realise that they are giving insights about life in their era for future generations.

Preserving Your Family History – An Act of Love

You do not need to be a great writer to write someone else's life story. This project can simply be an act of love, an opportunity to preserve family history. It is possible your parents or grandparents will never get around to completing this task themselves even with good intentions.

Oral history recording is flexible so that people of all ages can adapt a technique of asking, listening and researching. The treasures you discover from this project could enrich you and members of your family. Many people are concerned about "getting/doing it right". All that is required of you is to do your best.

Do Not Delay This Project

Our history depends upon human memory and the spoken word. As we get older often accurate memory recall is reduced.

The oral historian's anxiety syndrome is caused by the thought that valuable information could be slipping away. If you are going to accept the challenge and become an oral history writer do it sooner rather than later instead of waiting until a storyteller is in the latter stages of life.

Who Will Benefit From The Project?

The persons who may benefit the most could be the storyteller. It will not be a waste of time but a record of their life and times. As anyone reviews their life they are often amazed at what has been achieved and this can bring a sense of personal satisfaction.

The second person who will gain is the recorder as they discover stories that perhaps have never been told previously, and maybe see a different side to the person they thought they knew so well.

Ethical Issues: Boundaries, Trust, Confidentiality

Once parents agree to move forward with their oral history, boundaries need to be established. Before commencing, a combined list of subjects needs to be drawn up and agreed upon as a basis for discussion. Other topics can be added as the work progresses. To assist, several life history questionnaires follow at the end of this lesson that can be used as a starting point.

As the recorder, you will need to be careful not to intrude into someone's private territory, and to leave in the closet skeletons which might cause harm or embarrassment. Personal histories should be truthful, but individuals or families may prefer to leave some chapters closed where it is unnecessary to mention the information at all. The storyteller too needs to trust the recorder with the personal information they share. A strong bond can be achieved by emptying yourself of any expectations. Establish an adult/adult not a child/adult level of communication to help the parents to freely express their inner thoughts without censorship. Work at letting go of "parent labels". You are now two people with equal rights.

Agree that all material will remain confidential and the intellectual property of the parents. Options open to the parents:

1. The story may remain with the parents until death with an attached statement that copies could be made available to family members.

2. Parents may decide to publish their story immediately for family and friends.

Parent's Commitment – Life History Homework

Discuss what you require from your parents to make this project work. Several days prior to the interview, present your parents with a Life History Questionnaire so as to focus on issues you would like to discuss during the interview. This questionnaire is only meant as a basic guide to trigger thoughts. Preparation is the key to a successful interview and lack of preparation shows.

Do not let the interview be controlled by your Life History Questionnaire but use it as a starting point. Play your hunches and give your storyteller the freedom to explore other avenues.

Who cares if you only ask the first question on your list throughout the whole interview? If the interview lags or you get too far afield you can always go back to your list for inspiration or redirection. Do this in a gentle way that does not disrupt the story flow and upset the train of thought the storyteller is sharing. Be aware of meandering memories that do not appear to be going anywhere.

Agreement On Methodology

Agree on the best method suitable for the recording process.

1. Video recording – visual reaction to questions can be viewed.

2. Cassette recording – free to make notes but still hear their reactions.

3. Note taking (longhand or computer) - be an investigative journalist with an encouraging approach to subjects under discussion.

Decide on the number of interviews you think would be needed for the project. I suggest ten interviews of no more than two-hour duration over ten weeks. This will also depend on how well the interviews flow.

RECORDING SKILLS

Personal Preparation

Sufficient preparation by both parties spells the difference between a valuable and poor interview. Breaking the ice on arrival is an essential phase of helping the storyteller to become more comfortable by creating a relaxed environment. The best place for the interview to take place is usually in the storyteller's home where they are most comfortable to recapture old memories and their perceptions of events and experiences. Many people love to talk about themselves, what they did, where they lived and the things that happened to them.

Recorder

Do not use the interview to show off your knowledge, vocabulary or any other ability. The more relaxed you are the more relaxed your parents will be. Be organised and calm right from the beginning; be in control of the interview. Make sure any equipment used for recording is in working order prior to the meeting.

Storyteller/s

Allow time for the storyteller to become comfortable with the equipment you are using. Encourage them to have information available to refer to by using the Life History Questionnaire as a basic guide. Let them know they can refuse to answer questions at any time and that their wishes will be respected. Once you get past the simple niceties it is time to get down to business.

Keep It Simple – Where To Begin?

Begin where your parents want to start their story.

Start with questions that are not controversial; save delicate questions, if there are any, until you feel that you have earned trust and the storyteller is comfortable with the process. Be flexible. Watch for and pick up on promising topics. Progress is more important than perfection as you can put it together in logical sequence later.

Progress is made in short steps by encouraging and welcoming the information shared. Perhaps the storyteller is testing the recorder's reaction. Persistent gentle questioning evokes thoughts. "Do you remember anything else that relates to the situation…?" You are trying to extend their thinking.

Ask Simply Structured Open Ended Questions

Do not ask complicated multi-faceted questions. Ask brief, simple open-ended questions. You are seeking facts, feelings, stories and descriptions. Foster a spirit of co-operation with the way you ask questions e.g. "Could you tell me a little more about school days – education, games and sporting activities?"

Speak Calmly and Encouragingly

Even if you feel a little nervous, hide it. Create a relaxed atmosphere. Be in control of the interview without dominating. Show genuine interest in what your storyteller is sharing. Encourage them to speak freely.

Learning to Cope with Silence

Be aware there will be times when the storyteller needs to reflect on a question posed. Do not jump in and try to rescue them. Profound thoughts often come out of times of silence. Be comfortable and make silence your friend.

Do Not Sound Judgemental, Impatient, Disrespectful

Develop a non-judgemental attitude as you listen to the facts. Be patient if parents struggle with a reply to your question and show respect if your question is not understood. Accept responsibility for a poor question and rephrase it where necessary.

Leading Questions

Do not push for answers if a parent is unwilling to share. A loaded question puts words into the mouth of the storyteller which can produce an unfair comment which may not be truly in accord with their thinking.

Be Prepared to Abandon Your Plans

If you have selected a topic for the interview, be prepared to abandon your plans if a parent wishes to take the story in a different direction.

Human Minds Can Play Tricks

Do not challenge accounts that you think are inaccurate. Your parents may be telling you quite accurately what he/she believes they saw. The event is being recalled from their memory. At a later time after you have checked facts you could say, "I am not too clear about the particulars I recorded when...please help me to understand this event more clearly". Do not confront parents in a way to make them feel stupid; be sensitive to their feelings.

Recognise What Is Important

Notice when a story really grabs you as this could be an indication that it will be valuable to others. Take intelligent risks and explore these stories further. Listen to your gut reaction and recognise when you are on to something meaningful.

An Interview Is Not A Dialogue

You are there to collect facts not enter into a discourse. A good recorder does not dominate the interview but makes sure it is moving forward by asking intelligent questions at the right time. Michael Parkinson and Andrew Denton demonstrate this skill in their interviews. Encourage, guide, but do not push.

Recognise When The Storyteller Is Uncomfortable

Do not flee from difficult situations when the person becomes uncomfortable. Body language is a good indication. You are not there to rescue them. They have the right, which was established at the beginning, not to answer offensive or sensitive questions.

Fumbled Questions Put Storyteller At Ease

A fumbled question is one that is not clearly defined in the recorder's mind and is expressed in a clumsy and confusing manner but helps the storyteller to be at ease. Most of us do it naturally which gives the storyteller permission to fumble some replies too.

Avoid "Off The Record" Information

Recognise that human beings are complex. "Off the record" comments are stories or facts that the storyteller is prepared to share because a bond of trust has been established. This is privileged information and not to be made available to a wider circulation. Attempt to avoid these situations.

Be Aware Of Tiredness and Fatigue

If a person is showing signs of weariness and does not appear to be alert, be prepared to terminate the interview. An interview can be emotionally and intellectually draining.

Tracking Your Progress

Proceed step-by-step; as you discover problems during the process work through to find an acceptable solution without upsetting your parents. You will find that some people repeat themselves and leave out important facts so you need to review relevant questions. Recognise weaknesses in your interviewing skills and correct them. Review the "Seven Interviewing Skills For Researchers" in Lesson Two to help you. Some interviews will go better than others.

Establishing A Structure To Build Your Story

As you gather the story together you will begin to see a kind of scaffolding which produces a structure for your story. A theme starts to emerge as one gains experience in the art of listening and in trusting one's judgment.

Your parents have supplied the bare bones of their story and it is recorder's job to turn them into readable stories. Recognise patterns that are evolving in their story and steer them in the direction which will make the biggest impact.

In order for the structure to be reinforced oral history data must be subjected to the same test of evidence as other information. Check for accuracy as much as possible so that their story can stand up to the test of a social historian.

Write About Actual Experiences – Period of History

Actual experiences and events provide an insight into how your parents reacted in certain situations. It could be the arrival of their first child, a holiday that went terribly wrong or right, the loss of a child, a bankruptcy and other events. These are actual experiences and you, as the oral storywriter, need to understand their feelings and reactions.

If you are dealing with a period in our national history such as a war or economic recession there will be reliable information around to check the facts. In stories like these relate them to the way they affected your parents' life. Beware of too many generalities. New inventions, changing fashion, opportunities for learning can be turned into good stories.

People no longer write as many letters as they did in the past. Electronic communication has changed our world. Talk about the time before television and mobile telephones. The first family car can make a good story. Parents need trigger questions to help them to remember events of the past. Show how your parents reacted to their changing world.

POST INTERVIEW ACTIVITIES

Processing The Raw Material

All of these stories are grounded in memory which is a subjective instrument shaped by the present moment. It is the systematic collection of people's testimony about their own experiences.

After completing the agreed interviews you now have a rough draft. At this point you may feel overwhelmed with the size of the project. Be assured it will all come together.

Decide on the stories you will include in this oral history story and try to put them into logical sequence. Reveal how your parents did or did not adjust to the challenges life brought their way. Recognise contradictions in their story when interviewed separately. It does not mean someone is not telling "the truth". It goes to show how people experience events from their perspective. Try to establish the truth.

In some instances use the "generic person" e.g. "It is believed…" You could gently say, "Could you help me to clarify this story?"

Checking For Accuracy

You will not be able to cover every event in a storyteller's life. Select stories the person believes had a significant impact upon their life. You are reliant at this time upon the power of recall by the storyteller and how they witnessed the various events.

Their knowledge of their kith and kin often came from stories that were handed down to them, pictures of family gatherings and stories they have picked up along life's way.

As already stated, whether we like it or not we need to assess as far as possible the accuracy of the data gathered. We are not challenging the storyteller's honesty, more their power of recall. For example, actual dates of historical events can be checked. I have in my possession my birth certificate, my parent's wedding certificate, and my mother's death certificate. On each certificate my mother's age is cited at the time of those events. However working from the age given on each certificate she could have been born in three different years. A check of the Register of Births shows she was actually born in a different year altogether.

When recalling memories from a long-ago event, keep asking yourself how closely do the memories of the parent approximate a true rendering of the actual experience? At times, all you can do is accept the story as there is no way you can check its accuracy.

Questions of accuracy are not unique to this form of history taking. Problems of accuracy hound us no matter what source of historical data we use. People's perceptions of events are not foolproof. We view life's events from our own perspective. Make a comparison with data recorded from another interview. The transcript does not carry inflections of voice and body language. Readers will also add their own interpretation in trying to understand the conveyed message. As long as you are aware of the pitfalls you will have an eye to spot inaccuracies.

Present A Rough Draft

After you have finished processing the raw material and knocked it into a rough format present your story to the storyteller. It could stir further memories and gives them an opportunity to add or delete information if they wish.

Parents need to check names, dates, places and events. At this time they may wish to remove a story or two which they feel should not be included. If you disagree with their thinking you are allowed to have a say in the matter. The storyteller will make the final decision.

Writing The Story

After all the preliminary work has been done and the rough draft approved it is now time to write the story. Try and write in the way you think you parents speak, think and act - as a member of the family, you have a real advantage. After you have finished you may decide to seek the help of a professional editor to check the manuscript. Do not present the manuscript to your parents again until you are completely satisfied with your effort.

Completion Of Project

Feel proud of your achievement in this project. You have produced a valuable document. It is a gift you have given to your parents.

Should your parents wish their story to be published obtain information and costs for a self-publishing project with a small circulation for family and close friends. Encourage them to think about sending a copy to the National Library of Australia in Canberra, their State library and their local Municipal library. Biographical material is useful for researchers if there is reference to important events such as the Depression, world wars, environment issues, the Women's Movement and other national events that have influenced your parents' world.

With the finished document write a letter of appreciation for the parent's co-operation. Let them know how you have enjoyed the project and have come to know them far better. Reassure parents that it is their prerogative to decide what to do with their story.

LIFE HISTORY QUESTIONNAIRES

There is much more to writing someone's life history than simply listing names and dates. As you gather information you want the vital statistics, but also those little details that bring the story alive. For example, if Grandma had a pet, surely it had a name? How did she get it, who looked after it, where did it sleep etc? There are hundreds of questions that can be asked and each answer may suggest new questions. When you are really listening, you begin to ask why, how, who, when, where?

It is helpful to keep in mind that the following questions are a starting point only and serve basically two purposes: to gather or extend the information already known about a person or a period of time and to draw together a personal life history. In the historical sense some pieces of information will be more important than others but others will be more interesting. Refer to Lesson Two for ideas for more questions.

Life History Questionnaire No. 1

These are only thought starters to help the discussion move forward.

1. **Information About Your Father's Family**

   Family Facts: Where did they come from? Where did they live – city or country? What type of house was it? What work did your grandfather do? How many siblings did your father have? Where does your father fit in?

2. **Information About Your Mother's Family**

   Family Facts: Where did they come from? Where did they live – city or country? What type of house was it? What work did your grandfather do? How many siblings did your mother have? Where does your mother fit in?

3. **Father's Memories of Growing Up in Family Home**

   Childhood Memories: What are your earliest memories of your home? What did it look like? What was it made of? How many rooms did it have? Describe the rooms, the furnishings. Where did you sleep? Was there a garden – flowers, vegetables or fruit? Who looked after it? Were chickens or ducks kept? What family pets were there? What kind of meals did your mother cook? What was your parents' attitude to discipline? What rules governed the household? What part did church or religious activities play in your home? What family or neighbourhood gatherings do you recall?

4. **Mother's Memories of Growing Up in Family Home**

Childhood Memories: What are your earliest memories of your home? What did it look like? What was it made of? How many rooms did it have? Describe the rooms, the furnishings. Where did you sleep? Was there a garden – flowers, vegetables or fruit? Who looked after it? Were chickens or ducks kept? What family pets were there? What kind of meals did your mother cook? What was your parents' attitude to discipline? What part did church or religious activities play in your home? What family or neighbourhood gatherings do you recall?

5. **Influence of Grandparents**

Did grandparents live nearby? How often would they visit? How well did both families get on? Were grandparents supportive and helpful, or interfering? Did children visit grandparents for holidays? Were grandparents healthy and independent or dependent on parents?

6. **Other Important Facts About Grandparents**

Life History Questionnaire No. 2 - Family History

These are only thought starters to help the discussion move forward.

1. **Life For Dad Before Mum**

Describe your life with your siblings. Describe your home environment. School days: What schools did you attend? How far from home was your school? How did you get to school? What do you remember about your teachers? What kind of student were you? What subjects did you take? Who were your special playmates? What sport did you play? Describe playground games. How often or easily did you get into mischief? What discipline did you receive? Teenage years: what were your hobbies, interests, sporting or work activities? What level of schooling did you complete? How did you decide on the type of work you wanted to do? Describe your relationship with members of the opposite sex.

2. Life for Mum Before Dad

Describe your life with your siblings. Describe your home environment. School days: What schools did you attend? How far from home was your school? How did you get to school? What do you remember about your teachers? What kind of student were you? What subjects did you take? Who were you your special playmates? What sport did you play? Describe playground games. How often or easily did you get into mischief? What discipline did you receive? Teenage years: What were your hobbies, interests, sporting or work activities? What level of schooling did you complete? How did you decide on the type of work you wanted to do? Describe your relationship with members of the opposite sex.

3. Dad and Mum Meet

How and where did they meet? Was it love at first sight? Some stories from courting days. Any deep issues that needed to be faced e.g. religion, children, roles etc. Was there acceptance by parents? When and where were they married? Who were their attendants? Was it a traditional wedding? How did they dress? Are there any special stories from the honeymoon? Establishing their first family home together: Where did they choose to live? Was it a house or flat etc? What problems did they experience?

4. Let's Meet The Family

How many children in the family? Were there any family favourites? Were there any health or disability problems? Stories about the children: Any embarrassing moments?

What was the parents' attitude to parenthood? How did the family celebrate special family gatherings, birthdays, Easter, Christmas? Were there any special family observances?

5. **Stories Worth Telling**

    Was there a war, depression, natural disaster? Describe the effect upon your parents' relationship. Think of career pathways that may have challenged you. Were there any disappointments along the way? What fun times do you recall? Do you have any regrets? What proud moments do you recall?

6. **Other Important Issues**

Life History Questionnaire No. 3 - Family Activities

These are only thought starters to help the discussion move forward.

1. **Involvement In Community Activities**

    Were you active in service organisations such as Rotary, Lions Club etc, or on school committees, tuck shop, open days etc? How big a part did sport play in your family life? Were you involved as a coach, manager etc in the team? What about religious/church involvement? Did you have any affiliation with a political party?

2. **Memories From Family Holidays**

    Describe a family holiday you fondly remember. What about a family holiday that was disastrous? How did you decide where to go for holidays? Were children involved in deciding on the holiday destination? Did you go on holidays as a family or were others involved? Were holidays a highlight of your year?

3. **Hobbies And Activities**

    Describe your hobbies or activities. Did you excel in a hobby or sporting activity? Describe movies or entertainment you enjoyed. Did you play a musical instrument? What was a hobby or activity you would have liked to explore? Did you do any adult college courses?

4. **Attitude To Money**

    Did you find it difficult to make sufficient money to pay the bills? Were you good or bad money managers? What was your attitude to children's pocket money? Were there any inheritances or windfalls along the way?

5. **Social Interaction**

    What kind of social interaction with other family members and friends was there? How reserved or outgoing have you been? Were children's friends welcome at home? Did you include children in socialising activities?

Life History Questionnaire No. 4 - People Places Experiences

These are only thought starters to help the discussion move forward.

1. **Significant People Who Touched Your Life**

    How did your parents influence your thinking? Did grandparents take time to get alongside you? Was there any other friend or relative who helped you? Were you helped by a teacher, minister, or sporting coach? Was there an employer who helped you in your career?

2. **Significant Places You Have Visited**

    Describe a place you visited that is vivid in your memory. When were you here and for how long? Why is this place so clear? Who was there? What did you do? How long did you stay? What was your reason for visiting the place?

3. **Experiences That Have Made An Impact**

    Were you involved in a war or national disaster? Did you have some lucky escape? If you did, describe some of these events - even if painful. Are there significant highlights in your career that you would like to share? Were there any hard decisions you had to make? Is there a story or two you have never told?

4. **Roads Taken/Not Taken**

    Do you see yourself as having been an opportunity spotter? Do you like to play it safe? How did you decide on a career? What have you enjoyed most about your career? Did you have trouble finding the right path for career development? Did you travel along some dead-end roads that caused frustration? Are there opportunities that you feel you missed? If you could live life over again what changes would you make?

5. **Close Encounters of The Human Kind**

    How well did you relate to men and women? Do you consider yourself an introvert or an extravert? Do you find it easy to relate to people? Are you the life of the party? Do you regard yourself as a loner? How well do you communicate your needs to significant people in your life? Do you have close friends? Did you ever have a mentor or coach to confide in?

6. **Other Experiences Worth Sharing**

Life History Questionnaire No. 5 - Search For Meaning

These are only thought starters to help the discussion move forward.

1. **Values and Beliefs That Work Today**

    How have your values and belief changed over the years? How open are you to new thought? Do you respect others who differ in thought from you? Would you see yourself more tolerant now of others? What are your values and belief system based on?

2. **Sharing What Brings You Happiness and Joy**

    Do you feel you have found happiness and joy in your life? What brings you happiness? Do you regularly do what brings you happiness? Have you found happiness to be elusive at times? How do you show joy in your life? What has been the happiest moment in your life to date?

3. **Coping With Life's Cruel Blows**

    When life strikes a cruel blow how do you react or respond? Do you accept personal responsibility for your actions? What has been the toughest blow you have needed to face? What did you learn from the experience? Do you rise to a challenge or run away from it? Do you readily accept that change is part of life? Do you see yourself as a decision maker or procrastinator?

4. **What Are You Still Searching For?**

    Describe some of life's issues that concern you. What are you searching for at this time in your life? Are you gullible or do you question important decisions that affect our nation? What do you do to keep mentally alert?

5. **Sharing Lessons Learned From the School of Life**

What are some of the lessons you have learned from life's experiences? Sum up your personal philosophy in five concise statements.

6. **Other Insights**

WRITING EXERCISES FOR LESSON FOUR

1. Write a letter to your parents outlining the proposal to write an oral history. The letter should be about five paragraphs. Describe the benefits of the project.

2. Before commencing the project list stories you remember from your parent's life and check at the end if these are included in your parent's account.

3. List five stories that grab your attention in this list and analyse why you are drawn to these stories. Use these as a basis for your Life History Questionnaires.

Putting Pen To Paper

> *"If you read good books you will find*
> *good books will come out of you."*
>
> - Natalie Goldberg

Plan An Outline

Once you decide on what approach to use devise a general plan of how you will structure your story. Structure gives a sense of direction, and this is important for your readers to feel your story is going somewhere. Memories and events should have some connection for the story to flow. This plan need not be set in concrete. You will find that you will be continually revising it as you write. You might even find after writing your first draft you change the plan completely, but it is important to have a starting base.

Ready To Start Writing

If you feel a little overwhelmed by the challenge ahead of you, just break it up and focus on small parts such as individual topics within your chosen subject matter. Start where you feel most confident. It does not have to be at the very beginning.

Limit your writing at the beginning. Even twenty minutes to half an hour is a good starting point. Write for longer if you feel comfortable doing so, and if what you are writing seems to flow.

Write simply, as if you were speaking to a friend. Be chatty; choose words from your own vocabulary. Refrain from reviewing your work at this stage and do not be critical of what you have written. Your main aim at this point is simply to begin. A few completed pages will give you a sense of achievement and encouragement to continue.

A Suggested Strategy For Writing Your First Draft

One of the easiest ways to start writing is to follow an outline that divides your life into seven sections.

1. **Let's Meet The Family**

    Where did you live?

    Describe your home/neighbourhood.

    Describe your parents.

    Siblings.

    Your extended family.

    Family pets.

2. **Memories From Childhood**

    School days.

    Games you played.

    Friends you remember from school.

    Recreational interests – music, dance, sport, etc

    Religious activities.

Birthdays and special events.

What historical events do you recall from this period?

3. Adolescence

High school days.

Teachers.

Relationship with the opposite sex.

Learning to drive and getting your first car.

Alcohol, smoking, etc.

Cultural Issues.

What historical events do you recall from this period?

What effect did they have on you/ how did you respond?

4. Adulthood - Employment/ Higher Education

Choosing a career.

Training.

Periods of Unemployment.

Highlights from work.

Does this work still exist?

Any military service?

5. Enjoyment

Sporting activities.

Cultural activities.

Service organisations.

Religious activities.

Friendships and relationships.

Losses and disappointments.

Satisfying activities.

6. **Marriage and Family Matters, Divorce, Death**

> Courtship and marriage.
>
> High and low times.
>
> Children/grandchildren.
>
> Death of parent, sibling or child.
>
> Divorce and its consequences.
>
> Health matters.

7. **Life At This Time**

> Whether you are 30 or 70, describe your life at this time.
>
> Lessons worth sharing – things you have learned about life.
>
> Hopes, dreams and goals for the future.
>
> Attitude to ageing.
>
> Experiences worth sharing.

The strategy detailed here is a simple one as a guide, a sense of direction worth exploring.

Writing could stir up other memories and ideas. If the thought is not about what you are currently working on, jot it down in your Journal and develop the idea later. But at times a story will grab you and you will feel compelled to write about it. This may seem a fragmented approach but it is only your first draft, your first effort in writing your life story. You are sharing stories and experiences and feelings that are important to you at this time.

Get Your Rough Draft Down Quickly

Your rough draft is only for your eyes, so get it down quickly. It does not matter if it is contradictory, poorly expressed, or if the stories are in the wrong order. The aim is to get something down on paper. It does not matter about the length of the material. The important fact is that you have started – that's what counts. At this time you may not know where your story is going.

Twelve Tips For Writing Your First Rough Draft

1. Write your story your way. Put your imprint on your writing.

2. There is no time limit to complete your first draft.

3. Start your story at any time in your life. You can go back and fill in the details.

4. Be natural – write about what is important to you.

5. Free yourself from the need to be perfect. Your story is developing on paper and can be fine tuned later.

6. Be bold and adventurous. Write about how things were, not how you wish them to be.

7. You are reviewing your life to share with a reader. Allow your first draft to find your story.

8. Do not worry about what you have written and how it sounds.

9. Share experiences that have shaped your life.

10. Use the shortest words and the simplest sentences that convey your meaning.

11. Think of writing as simply telling a story.

12. No one can tell your story better than you. Write from your perception of self – not what others have told you.

Reviewing Your Rough Draft

Your first draft is for your eyes only. Keep remembering the word "rough" - that is what it is - scattered thoughts about your life. Some thoughts you will eliminate others you will build upon.

See if you can recognise a theme evolving. Read your writing aloud. Is it tedious, dull or boring, or is it alive and exciting? If necessary, rethink your approach. There may be many drafts before you discover what you really want to say.

Example

I have been described by some of my friends as a rough and ready character. I think I pick up some of this from my father. I am not good at attention to detail. A rough draft is simply writing down scattered thoughts without too much thought about sequence, structure or grammatical correctness. I wrote six rough drafts and threw them all away until I felt the last had the makings of what I wanted to say.

Summary: Remember that the first draft will not resemble anything like the finished manuscript. It is rough and unpolished, but it contains the elements of a good story. In your rough draft you have complete freedom so do not be afraid to write what you might think is rubbish. Do not censor your work at this stage.

WRITING EXERCISES FOR LESSON FIVE

1. Using the "Suggested Strategy For Writing Your First Draft" create a basic outline for your first draft.

2. Write freely and do not censor any errors.

3. After you have finished your first draft, put it away for a few days before reading it aloud to yourself.

4. Whether you have written two pages or twenty or more, give yourself a pat on the back for what you have achieved.

5. Your next step. After reading your first draft, you may decide on a new course of action. Here are a few suggestions worth considering.

    Join a writers group for support and encouragement.

    Enrol in a writing course which will assist you with this project.

    Visit a library and read a book on creative writing or simple rules for English expression.

    Select an autobiography and study the approach used by the author. Look for ideas that may be helpful for you.

    Put your manuscript away for two or three weeks and then revisit it.

    Expect to write two, three or more drafts before you proceed further. It is a way to sort out what you really want to include.

Once you have started writing and getting into the flow, exercise patience and persistence.

Basic English Expression

*"You don't write because you want
to say something, you write because
you have something to say."*

- F Scott Fitzgerald

The Basics

Without basic knowledge of grammar, punctuation and word usage you will have difficulty communicating. Once you understand the basic rules of grammar and how language works, you will recognise the part each word plays in your sentence.

Grammar is the arrangement, relationships, and functions of words and the ways they are put together to form phrases, clauses, or sentences.

Punctuation marks are signals which help readers to understand the ideas in a passage and to read more quickly and efficiently.

Usage is the way in which words and phrases are actually used, spoken, or written.

Do a refresher course in English expression if you are not certain of the basic rules of grammar. You need to understand how words work. The right grammatical choices influence the impact of your writing.

Parts Of Speech

Parts of speech are the fundamental building blocks of traditional grammar, and explain the ways words can be used in various contexts.

Noun: A noun is a word that can be used to refer to a person, place or thing.

Verb: A verb expresses action. (He *jumped*.) It also expresses a state of being. (She *will be* here soon.)

Pronoun: A pronoun can replace a noun or pronoun. (Sara found *her* book.)

Adjective: An adjective is used to describe or modify nouns. (She is a *pretty* girl.)

Adverb: Describes or limits verbs, adjectives, and other adverbs. (They run *quickly*.)

Preposition: A preposition is a word used to relate a noun or pronoun to some other part of the sentence. (My cat is *on* the chair.)

Conjunction: A conjunction links words, phrases, or clauses. (Mary *and* I went to the movies.)

Interjection: An interjection is a word added to a sentence to convey emotion. (*Oh no*, what will Mary think?)

Sentence Structure

Sentences express a complete idea and have a subject and predicate.

A **predicate** is the part of a sentence which tells what the subject does or is or what is done to the subject.

Phrases are groups of related words which are missing either a subject or a predicate.

Clauses are groups of related words, with a subject or predicate, which form sentences when joined by conjunctions.

A sentence should contain no unnecessary words. Strive for simplicity and naturalness of expression. Believe that less is more.

The Paragraph

A paragraph consists of a number of sentences grouped together to discuss one main subject. The first sentence will convey the topic, followed by supporting sentences, and then a concluding sentence.

The main function of the paragraph is to help your readers understand what you are saying. It gives structure by *organizing* the information in a logical manner. When you begin a new idea, it is time to start a new paragraph. Each paragraph focuses on one topic or idea. Occasionally, related ideas may be grouped into a single paragraph if they each take only a sentence or two to explain. In general, though, one idea/topic equals one paragraph.

Punctuation

Punctuation marks are signals to your readers. In speaking, we can pause, stop, or change our tone of voice. In writing, we use punctuation to emphasize and clarify what we mean.

Apostrophe: An apostrophe tells the reader that a word is either a possessive or a contraction. A contraction is simply two words collapsed into one. (can not > can't, it is > it's). The possessive tells the reader that someone or something owns or possesses the thing that comes after the possessive. (Graham's car)

Colon: Use a colon before a list (We need three ingredients: flour, milk and eggs.), or a summary (To summarise: spelling and punctuation are important elements of writing.)

Semi-colon: The semi-colon is used to join together two independent clauses, that is, two clauses that could be sentences but have some relationship. (Sarah is not a good typist; she makes many mistakes.)

Comma: The comma tells the reader to pause. Place a comma between a list of three or more words. (Up, down, left and right.) Use a comma to give additional information (Mr Hardy, from England, was my maths teacher.) Use a comma when *but* or *for* is used. (I did my best, but the rules are hard to follow.) There are many rules for the use of a comma, but basically it is used when a pause is required to make reading more natural and to avoid confusion about what is being said. Read your work aloud and you will get a good idea where to place it.

Quotation Marks: Use quotation marks for direct speech. (Graham asked, "Do you understand?")

Exclamation Mark: Use an exclamation mark for emphasis. (I loved the book!) Be careful of overuse.

Question Mark: Use a question mark when you pose a direct question. (May I see your book?)

A Full Stop: Use a full stop to end all other sentences. (This is the end of the lesson.)

Overuse of punctuation slows continuity. The grammar check on word processors is useful for checking your work. However, read the rule carefully and make sure it applies to what you have written.

Words Are Your Tools Of Trade

Word usage can either make or break a story. By choosing carefully, you can find words to clearly communicate your meaning, tone, and purpose. Learn to use the right words to express your thoughts as they create the mood and atmosphere for your life story. Keep reading other works and see how the authors use words. Always have a dictionary and thesaurus by your side, and use them. The selection of inappropriate words may cloud or obscure the meaning you wish to convey.

Avoid Clichés Where Possible

Clichés stand in for more precise descriptions of something. Clichés are often used because we are too lazy to put the message in a format which is more relevant. Use words to excite, impress, involve, shock and amuse the reader. Slow down and write exactly, precisely what you mean. Use fresh vibrant words rather than clichés. If you get stuck ask yourself why or how?

Using Adjectives And Adverbs Sparingly

Use adjectives and adverbs sparingly to add colour to your story. The message the words are conveying has to be clear. If a word jumps out of the page for no apparent reason, it could be distracting from the story.

Identify Favourite Word Syndrome

When editing your manuscript, be aware of the overuse of certain words or phrases. Use your thesaurus to find replacement words. Having another person read your manuscript will more easily help recognise these words.

Dealing With Numbers

Numbers between one and ten can be written in words but thereafter digits are used. In writing a date put the month first followed by the exact day and year e.g. January 1, 2004. Do not insert "th" after the day.

Historical Dates

If you are going to discuss historical events be sure to check and recheck dates. Do not be lazy and pluck the date from the air without doing your research. Quote your source of reference. Seek help from your local librarians. Tell them what you are doing and you will find that they will go out of their way to help you.

The Right Words For Historical Settings

As you describe items and events from a different period use the appropriate words

e.g. "radio" "wireless". Many years ago there were no washing machines and the ladies of the time used to boil their clothes in a "copper", used a "washboard" to scrub them, and then hung their washing on the clothes line supported by wooden "props".

Writing In The First Person

Writing is simply speaking on paper. Most life stories are written in the first person. Initially, you might find it difficult using "I" so much. It is hard to avoid, as you are writing about yourself, but you will soon feel comfortable. A well-written life story will sound like the author speaking. In speech "I" is acceptable. A person writing in the third person sounds stilted and uncomfortable. It appears that you are trying to hide yourself.

Checking A Statement

To test a statement in your story – ask the question "Does it make sense?" If no, rewrite it. Then ask "Is this relevant?" If "No", omit it. Then "And does it make sense?" If it is relevant, ask the next question.

Overstatement/Understatement

Overstatement occurs when too much detail is given and it is hard to comprehend the significance of what is written. It gives the story a slant that does not necessarily reflect the true facts. Overstatement is a way to cover up undesirable facts or colour them in such a way that the message is not clear.

Understatement occurs when the writer has limited information available and there is only a sketchy presentation of basic facts. It can also occur when the writer assumes the reader knows all the facts and therefore parts of the story are omitted. The writer should never presume that the reader is acquainted with the necessary facts.

Writing Rules Can Broken

Once you understand the basic rules of writing you are free to break them but need to be willing to accept criticism over them. Know that verbs move your story along especially if they relate to an action taken by your character. The written word has permanence more so than the spoken word. The spoken word can be changed immediately if it needs to be corrected. It is harder to correct the written word. Newspapers frequently publish a short paragraph heading "corrections" but it is impossible to do this with a "one-off effort".

How All This Information Will Help You

Every writer needs an understanding of the basic rules. Knowing the rules helps you to get your message across clearly.

Simple rules of syntax, i.e. grammar, sentence structure and language rules help you to organise your thoughts and explain yourself to others.

The right word, the right expression, gives voice to your inspiration. Word by word your story unfolds.

Words are your tools; the rules of grammar are your blueprint.

Punctuation marks are like road signs placed along the highway to control our speed of explanation.

Keep asking yourself is the vocabulary accurate, varied and complies with the basic rules of writing so to engage the reader.

You can never know too much as a writer – there is always something new to learn.

You learn to be a writer by doing it. The rules are there to help you, not hinder you.

Make no excuses for poor writing, but be true to yourself and feel that you have written to the best of your ability.

Ernest Hemingway said, "Be an honest writer and be true to yourself."

You Do Not Have To Be An Expert In English Expression

Understand the nature of your audience and communicate with sincerity and authority; put yourself in the place of an interested reader. Use grammar to the best of your ability, but don't get bogged down in the mechanics of it all. In the main, you have a tolerant readership that is prepared to accept some grammatical errors. Take time to reflect on what you have written and see if it could be presented more clearly. People want to experience your enthusiasm more than your grammatical correctness.

This has been just a brief review of the basics of grammar. If you feel you need to do additional reading there are many books available at your local library or in bookshops.

WRITING EXERCISES FOR LESSON SIX

1. What is your reaction to this short course in English expression – describe your thoughts in 50 words or less.

    If you feel this lesson has stirred up conflicts within you that relate to writing put them down on paper and note what you can do to improve the situation.

Now with this new knowledge go back through your first rough draft and make any grammatical corrections you feel necessary. Do not rewrite your rough draft. Make corrections only.

The Writing Craft – Style Structure, Voice, Pacing

"Every writer I know has trouble writing."

- Joseph Hiller

Learning The Writing Craft

People who enjoy arts and craft recognise they first need to learn some basic skills. Once they do this they are free to put their own mark upon their work as their ability and confidence develops. The same message applies to the writer. With basic knowledge he/she will develop the skills to write in a way that best expresses thoughts, personality and character.

Understanding Basic Writing Requirements

Some writers may feel intimidated by this lesson, as all they want to do is to write their life story without learning too much about the writing craft. They might feel all that "stuff" is for the professional writer. However, by understanding style, structure, voice and pacing, you will discover ways to write which brings some polish to your manuscript. This helps it to be more readable and to have a greater impact.

Craft and Characterisation

There will be many characters in your life story. By improving your knowledge of the writing craft you are able to bring those characters alive by using the right language that presents an accurate description e.g. "Bill was an argumentative character who could stir the group. Once the group discussion flowed he would sit back and enjoy the encounter. Yet Bill had another side to his character that when people needed help, he was the first to offer." Showing more than one side of Bill creates more interest. If we just spoke of the quarrelsome side to his nature we would actually give the wrong impression of the person.

Build Believable Characters

Each of your characters has some distinctive qualities. Describe them in your writing. Here are a few suggestions to think about: describe good and bad qualities, demeanour, whether strong, gentle or weak, approximation of age, culture, speaking style and other important personality traits.

Translating Your Thoughts Into Words

In writing, you are translating thoughts, ideas and experiences that are important to you. You have to work out how to put your thoughts down on paper in a way so they can be clearly understood. You do this by choosing the right words that accurately describe the circumstances.

Precise Writing Is Hard Work

It is far easier to write a thousand words than five hundred that still aptly describes an experience. Learn to condense a story without losing its meaning. When you ramble you are wasting words. Keep in mind the purpose of the story you are sharing. Any unrelated information detracts from your story.

STYLE

Understanding Style

The style a writer uses tells us something of his spirit, his way of life, his ability to do or experience things; it reflects his personality. Although many books give tips on how to get your thoughts on paper no one set of rules has been devised to suit everyone. There is no perfect guide to good writing, just as there is no guarantee that a person who thinks clearly will be able to communicate clearly on paper. Our style emerges and develops as we become more skilled in the use of language. Writing is sometimes hard work and success comes through persistence, and trial and error.

Your Style Can Help Your Story Live Forever

There are no magical formulae to engage your reader to help your story live forever. Readers feel your presence through your words and style which reflects the genuineness and authenticity about what you are saying. Your story and style engages the reader whether it is through a concept or thought you wish to convey.

Write Naturally

Write naturally using words you are familiar with and that come easily to you. Write clearly to communicate your story. Your personality and your voice will be seen in your writing. Your readers will feel that you are sharing yourself and your insights; this comes not only through your content but the emotional tone of your writing.

Example

It is 6 pm on an Easter Thursday in 1953 and I am on my way to a youth camp I had organised as a young student minister. I was driving a 1929 Chevrolet 4 overloaded with bedding, mattresses, supplies and the "kitchen sink" across the Capalaba bridge which joined Brisbane with Redland Bay, a popular holiday area of the time just south of the city. The ropes broke and my load spilled out onto the bridge blocking it in both directions. There was chaos until the police arrived. They were not too happy with me and soon commandeered a nearby truck. The truckie, "my guardian angel", quickly had all my supplies and equipment on the back of the truck and set off for the camp site. The old Chevie then failed to start and had to be pushed off the bridge.

Summary: A story simply told that some people could relate to quite easily. Packing for a holiday, a busy road and disaster happens but is quickly helped by the intervention of police and a passing driver.

Writing From Your Perspective

You may learn much about yourself through writing your life story. It could be quite revealing to discover how you reacted in certain situations.

You are the expert on your life. You have a wealth of experience locked away inside of you which will be revealed in the stories you share.

Using Evocative and Expressive Words

These are words that you use in everyday conversation with family and friends. Evocative words are used to obtain a reaction. You may evoke a response by making a statement e.g. a discussion about the condition of the world and evoke a response to the question posed.

You may use expressive words to back up a statement. You could use "the world is hell bent on destruction". This is another way to emphasise your concern as it builds intensity into your story. It shows you have a strong conviction about what is being discussed and you are prepared to do something about it.

Using these evocative and expressive words shows your passion and concern. Perhaps it also shows you in a new light.

Example

On our trip around Australia Carmel and I took a day tour from Kununurra to the El Questro Tourist & Cattle Ranch in northern Western Australia. We looked forward to our little expedition to this legendary ranch on a typical hot sunny day during the tropical north "dry" season. Although we were told we could make it to the ranch ourselves in our little Toyota Corolla sedan, the four wheel drive we were in took an hour to cover the 25 kilometres stretch of the dusty, rutted, potholed famous Gibb River Road.

Having reached our destination and recovered from our jarring drive, thankful we did not bring our little car, we decided to go for a walk along the creek with the others on the tour. It was described by our guide as an "easy" walk although there would be some rocks to climb over. Half way along the terrain became rougher, the rocks became boulders and the going got considerably tougher, especially for Carmel. The guide made it clear that he was not there to help any of us up and over the boulders; we had to rely on our partners only. The heat and exertion combined soon made Carmel exhausted and we stopped and after a rest returned to the station homestead. It was a slow nightmare of a journey back and Carmel was as white as a ghost, but she was determined to get there before the others returned. With the help of a sugar based drink from the bar she gradually recovered.

We learnt very quickly to question carefully what others call "easy". And thankfully our young guide was the only one on our wonderful three month long trip that lacked sensitivity and care for his charges.

Summary: What started as a simple travel story turned into a dramatic tale. The story indicates our predicament with no help from the tour guide. The nightmare of the journey back is not described but left to the reader's imagination. The story evolves and suggests a sense of helplessness as the facts are described - the terrain, boulders and intense heat of the outback and the lack of care of the guide.

Sprinkle Details

Learn to sprinkle details through your story. Too much detail at the beginning can confuse the reader. Sprinkle details in such a way that the reader is hungry to discover more. By using this approach characters and events appear on the page in easy to understand segments. If you provide too much, too early, the reader may feel there is not need to read any further or give up because they feel saturated with too much detail.

Example

Sylvia, a young woman in prison, heard me interviewed on Radio 2GB. Two years later she arrived on my doorstep asking for counselling. She was angry and hurt and I believed wrongly imprisoned. Just skin and bone she was very fearful, jumpy like a frightened animal. She at first gave me a false name, address and telephone number and said, "I am going to tell you nothing". After a silence of 30 minutes I opened my office door and said, "Be free to go at anytime". Another 20 minutes went by and Sylvia started to cry and then the session really began.

After several interviews counselling reached a stalemate. I decided to take an unusual step and introduce Sylvia to the family and the children soon grew to love her for she played with them. They corrected her table manners, her rude expressions, and cared for her and gradually Sylvia changed. On her 35th birthday the children arranged her first ever birthday party which made Sylvia very emotional but was a great success. The children did more for Sylvia than my psychological counselling.

Summary: There was an inner compulsion in me that I knew the story needed to be told. Sylvia's story is a success story not because of me but because of my children – John, Ruth and Andrew. Here I have exposed my children and given the reader a little more insight. I write from my perspective when I say "I believe she was wrongly imprisoned". I use conjecture as I learn about the facts of the case. I sprinkle scant details to protect her privacy. The story ends with a "feel good factor".

Make A Good Impression

The first sentence, paragraph and chapter of your story need to grab the readers' attention and make a favourable impression. It helps them to think and feel you have something worthwhile to say. Also to arouse the readers' curiosity, some writers tantalise them with unusual chapter headings. The full meaning of the chapter titles is often not revealed until the end.

Style And Balance Go Together

Your style is reflected by maintaining a balance between seriousness and fun, success and failure. Life is never all bad or all good. Life is bittersweet. We sometimes have a tendency to forget the fun experiences and concentrate on life's problems.

Difference Between Show And Tell

There is only a subtle difference between show and tell. You demonstrate to the reader your characters by the way you describe their actions and insight into their personality and qualities. You present to your reader an image they can accept or reject.

In the telling you draw your own conclusions and inform the reader what you believe are the fundamental facts based on your observations. Telling the reader is taking away their personal freedom to make up their own minds about characters.

Show The Reader What Is Happening

Show the reader what is happening so that it feels real to him. For example you may mention a room you entered which is central to what is to follow. Take time to introduce the reader to the room and describe some of the décor before going on with the core of the story.

STRUCTURE

Understanding Structure

Structure is the framework of your book; the way you want your story to unfold. For writing to be productive and effective a basic structure is required.

Laying The Foundation For Your Writing

A house builder starts off with a plan drawn up by an architect. Through the sketches and drawings he has a vision of what the house will look like when completed.

The same is true in writing your life story. Writers build a story in a similar way a builder constructs a house – piece by piece. You start with sketchy ideas - rough drafts - and eventually a solid structure for your story forms.

Developing Story Sequence

One thought leads to another, and before you realise what is happening you have a series of stories coming together in logical sequence. You know what ideas you need to develop next in your story, a series of links that hold your story together. When your manuscript is in the editing stage you may discover that a section fits better in another chapter. It can be easily transferred.

Writing your life story is like putting a jigsaw puzzle together. Once you have established a story sequence the pieces will come together.

Add A Touch Of Drama

Important pivotal experiences often happen in a dramatic way. Firstly create the scene and allow the drama to evolve. Build excitement, tension and add a twist if possible to your story. Drama can bring with it a thrill or journey into the unknown.

Example

I will never forget one Sunday morning my encounter with a disturbed man holding a nine-inch knife pointed at my chest. In an unscheduled counselling interview he gave me an account his problem and what he had done. I told him the action he had taken was stupid and he had to be responsible. My badly chosen words pushed the man too far and he pulled out his knife. He said if I repeated that statement again he would kill me, and I knew he meant it. After a while I convinced him to put the knife on the desk and he agreed to see a doctor. That afternoon on his way back from Yeppoon, a Rockhampton seaside resort, he had an accident and killed three nurses who I knew at the Rockhampton General Hospital. He was not seriously hurt. Out of that ghastly experience I realised I needed a lot more training in counselling.

Summary: The story starts with a dramatic introduction which grabs the reader and continues through the story. It soon becomes evident that I am out of my depth in counselling and there is a struggle to get control of the interview. I introduce a guilt factor, expressed with the death of the three nurses. It was a major turning point in my life.

Choosing The Right Stories To Tell

The right stories do not have to be dramatic or headline catching. You will know through intuition that the stories you are about to tell are right and need to be told. A good criterion in deciding which stories to use is to ask this question "If I leave out a particular story will it affect the rest of my writing?" If there is any doubt, don't use it. The stories you use helps the progression of your main theme.

Example

I was "King of the Poo" when I developed a thriving business at eight years of age. I sold a sugar bag of manure collected in the local paddocks for a sixpence. I would regularly take in about ten shillings a week, which added up to a lot of poo. As we were very poor the money was given to my parents for food and schoolbooks. It was depression time and my father was out of work for six years.

Being of an enterprising nature I decided to extend my "business empire" and collect meat orders from neighbours on Friday mornings and deliver them in the afternoon after school. I now doubled my income with tips from the neighbours and a few shillings from the butcher. My business came to an abrupt end one hot summer's day as I left the filled meat orders in "the poo cart" while I went to play with some mates. By the time I delivered the meat it was not fit for human consumption. Not to be beaten, I bought day old chicks, fattened them up in the back yard, Dad cut off their heads, Mum cleaned them and I sold them. A new business emerged.

Summary: My success and failures in business are told here in an entertaining manner. The facts are clear. My unique voice comes through in the story ("King of the Poo") and the description that follows. It is a story that reveals the real self who was later to emerge as an astute businessman.

Following An Underlying Theme

The structure of your story becomes clear when you are mindful of the theme or point you wish to make. Make sure the stories you are sharing clearly relate to the chapter and the underlying theme. If you are writing about parents deal with stories that are connected with their basic beliefs, your changing relationship with them, and your home environment.

Revising Your Structure

Take time to revise the structure of your story, but wait until you have finished writing before you do so. Premature editing can kill your story. Rearrange the contents if necessary to improve story flow.

There will be times of internal wrestling - deciding which aspects of your journey need to be told. The right structure gives your story direction and creates a sense of momentum.

Stick To The Point

Complete one point at a time. Avoid potential reader confusion; do not allow your thoughts to jump around the page. Stick to the point under consideration before proceeding to the next one.

Know when you have finished. Make sure that your explanation is clear. This prevents you from being guilty of misinterpretation of facts.

Build Intensity Into Your Story

Allow your story to build in strength. Write with passion and conviction whether it is a joyful or painful experience. Pass the excitement onto the reader by communicating the intensity and emotions of the incident as if it were happening at the moment.

Example

I am sitting in a coffee shop in Margaret Street, Sydney with tears rolling down my cheeks. A lady at a nearby table observes me and asks if she can sit with me. No words are spoken. After 30 minutes my "guardian angel" leaves. She pays for my coffee.

I had just attended an Elizabeth Kluber-Ross seminar on death and dying with 200 people who seemed excited by the presentation. It was the only time in my life when I felt severely depressed and it was a week before I came to realise the reason for this. Certainly the seminar on death made me face my own mortality, the certainty that I will eventually die. But it was more than this. Then I remembered Kluber-Ross' words "Our concern must be to live while we are alive – to release ourselves from behind the façade designed to conform to external definition of who and what we are". It had occurred to me then that I had never really lived, only existed.

Summary: The emotion of sadness turns into depression. The reader discovers what I was feeling. The introduction into the story of my hero "the guardian angel" brings a true sense of pathos as not a word is spoken. My point of enlightenment after seven days brings relief. The suspense factor is used to leave the reader guessing how this affected my life.

Lost The Plot?

Keep in mind the reason you are writing your life story and what you wish to convey. This helps you to keep your writing on track. You may appear to have lost the plot when your story wanders and there seems to be no logical structure holding it together.

Have you gone off on a tangent? You need to be aware of the reason you are telling this story at this point. Sometimes we need to explain a situation by going backwards or forwards in time; or to introduce a person who had some influence over you or the situation. Another reason is to show a side of your character which you believe is not properly understood and is necessary in appreciating your response to what you are writing about. But if it doesn't seem to fit just leave it until you finish writing and deal with it later.

Also, when your story appears to be vague or contradictory it is an indicator that there is some confusion in your thinking. This could be caused by insufficient research, tiredness, or fearfulness about what you are trying to share. Again, leave it until you finish writing and then revise it.

Beginning, Middle And Ending

The majority of books, plays and films have a beginning, middle and an ending. There are some exceptions to the rule. Some will leave you in suspense if there is to be a sequel.

The beginning of your life story needs to grab attention. This can be achieved through creating curiosity, conflicting impressions or a startling statement.

The middle has to do with regulating the pace and momentum. At times your pace will be slow and at other times it will be lively. To achieve this goal the writer must generate interest by the imaginative portrayal of the saga of events.

The ending needs to wrap up your story. If possible try to end your story on a positive note. As your life continues to evolve indicate there could be more to follow. Some writers conclude with their homespun philosophy and how it helped them to cope with life.

Knowing How and When To End Your Story

Although ideas are still coming to you try to end your story with the thought readers may still want to know more. You life still continues to evolve. There could even be a sequel to follow, or an epilogue that brings the reader up-to-date with your current world.

VOICE

Understanding Voice

In writing, voice is the way your writing *sounds* on the page. It is the way you write, the tone you take - friendly, formal, chatty, or distant - the words you choose, the pattern of your sentences, and the way these things fit in, or not, with the style of your story. It is the unique way you put words on the paper that makes your writing distinct from other authors.

Finding Your Writer's Voice

Your writing voice should be an expression of your personality, one that when you read your manuscript aloud sounds like you. Keeping a journal is an excellent way to find your voice. Knowing we are the only ones who will ever read the words on a journal page we can feel free to experiment. Voice is a way you project yourself through your writing and when you first start this may appear to be tentative. As you pick up the momentum your voice tone will change.

Reading Your Story Aloud

One of the best ways to listen to your voice is to read your writing aloud. Experiment with different styles. Different kinds of writing may reveal different aspects of your own voice. Try comedy or mystery writing as an exercise.

Movement

As a writer you can move around in your story from the past to the present to the future. You can challenge the reader, surprise them with your activities, exaggerate your story or leave a question unanswered.

Write The Way You Speak

Write the way you speak so that your reader will instantly see you saying the words. When you are describing sad or joyful expression use words that come easily to you, and that help the reader to experience what is happening at this moment.

Your Public and Private Voice

You have two voices - a public and a private one. Your public voice may sound much different from your private voice. Study this comparison and present a believable voice tone. This can be well illustrated with reference to a comedian. The private voice of the comedian can be soft and reserved. Place a script in front of the comedian and his voice changes together with his personality.

PACING

How To Pace Your Story

Through the craft of writing you gain an understanding about the power of language. You learn that padding your story slows it down. Feelings and actions in your story increase its intensity. Curiosity holds reader interest in what will happen next.

The right pacing keeps a story moving forward. It allows your story to move freely from point to point without a jarring effect.

Pacing And Story Flow

You can slow your story down or increase its momentum by regulating the pace. At times your pace will be slow as you are dealing with major events and at other times it will be lively and chatty when writing about bits of trivia.

The major and the minor events bring about contrast in your story. There could be a tendency to skim over minor events and focus on the major ones. Often what you consider to be minor events of your story are significant to your reader.

Story Hooks

A dominant theme that runs through your chapter can produce a chapter title. It is like the skeletal frame which holds the body together. Through personal and intimate stories the writer is able to hook the reader through curiosity. Posing a question at the end of a chapter and not fully answering it hooks the reader into the next chapter.

Building and Maintaining Momentum

Short crisp clear sentences build momentum. Eliminate unnecessary adjectives and adverbs. Drop out superfluous words. Use active voice which is more vigorous and direct. *I shall always remember my first love*, rather than *My first love will always be remembered by me*. Make definite statements, and avoid colourless, tame or vague language.

WRITING EXERCISES FOR LESSON SEVEN

1. Now that you are half way through this book, take time to structure the contents of your story. Think of chapter headings or topics which you would like to share.

2. Now make a list of the chapters and decide in what order they are to appear in your story.

3. Refer to research material from your Jottings Journal and decide upon the stories you wish to share.

4. With this framework of reference write your second draft - its could be longer than your first. This writing experience could take a considerable period of time. It is wise to limit your writing to two hours per day and then stop.

5. After completing your second draft, leave for seven days before reading again.

How To Connect With Your Reader

"The role of the writer is not to say what we all say, but what we are unable to say."

- Anais Nin

Develop A Lively, Chatty Style

A chatty style never seems to fail to connect with the reader. Using your own voice, basically writing as you speak, is like engaging in a one on one conversation. The personality of the writer soon becomes evident. The lively style keeps the story moving at a good pace. As you work on, adding your voice to your stories, be sure to strive for natural conversational tones and patterns.

Prior Knowledge of The Story Teller

Writing down your own life story is a great way to preserve precious family memories and create a living record of history that can be enjoyed by countless generations to come. No doubt your close family and friends would make up your major readership. These friends are very supportive and keen to know you better. Others with only a little knowledge of you might also like to read your story.

When the storyteller is known - a celebrity or public figure - there can be heightened reader interest. It is human nature that we form impressions and make judgements about people. When a person writes a life story it gives the reader an opportunity to test these impressions. Many people hide their real identity behind a façade. This façade could have been used as a means of defence or protection, so unless this causes unnecessary trauma, consider allowing the reader to see the real you, write with honesty.

New Readers

For new readers there will be players who they do not know. Take time to show who they are, how they fit into your life and the effect they had upon you. Although they may only appear fleetingly in your story, make it obvious why they have been included.

People Love A Good Storyteller

Do you have a reputation as a teller of yarns? Do people come to rely on you for stories? The majority of people love a good storyteller and this is an excellent way to make connection as you share an experience from your life. Take time to create the scene before your character appears. After you share the experience discuss how you reacted by showing the feelings or thoughts it aroused. Let the reader see the purpose for recounting a particular event and how it fits in to the rest of your narrative.

Sharing Life's Full Spectrum

Be prepared to share your joy, happiness and successes as well as your disappointments, sadness, failures, pain and frustration. By doing this you are presenting a balanced picture. Write about the simple everyday situations as well as the profound experiences. Life is made up of "highs and lows". Share how you felt on these occasions. Think about the knowledge you gained from each of these experiences and with hindsight see how you could have handled them differently.

Have Something Worthwhile To Say

Believe you have something worthwhile to share. It could relate to your value judgements or discoveries you have made about yourself and life. It does not matter how old or young you are, your standard of education, your conventional or unconventional way of life, your experiences have helped to make you who you are today. Consider your audience; give thought to what you want to say. Why is it important for you to share your story? What message do you want to convey? If you wish to make a provocative statement, be prepared to back it up, but remember that even the ordinary events of life can capture the attention of the reader.

Make Your Reader Think – Challenge Preconceived Opinions

When you challenge preconceived ideas you cause the reader to rethink the event or the experience if it was known to them. This is a way of connecting with the reader as you challenge their opinions. The reader engages with you based on his knowledge of the event and any new information you present.

Through your honesty in writing you can challenge opinions by presenting your account of a story. To challenge does not necessarily mean change will take place. It is a way to present facts that the reader may not have been aware of which may shed new light on the incident. The reader may agree or disagree about the information but at least has taken time to rethink the experience.

Some writers, with a chip on their shoulder, keep stirring the pot of memories and challenge the reader too much. This writing approach becomes offensive and serves no worthwhile purpose.

Allow Your Writing To Move You

If your writing moves you, it is very likely it will have a deep impact upon your reader. No one can teach you how to do it, and there will be plenty of times when you will struggle to find the right words. Readers want more than historical and chronological facts. They want to feel and share your life's experiences. What keeps your reader engaged from the beginning is the tension created by the conflict between desire and the resolution, a question begging to be answered. Will the girl get the guy? Who-dun-it? Will the hero reach his/her goal? You create the tension by the way you go about recounting your story.

Evoke Readers' Emotions

The appearance, words and nature of your story must be vivid and understandable for the reader to identify with and be moved by a life experience. Share intimate feelings, paint the picture. Create the action of cause and effect with images and sounds gradually mounting intensity to the climax, and finally the conclusion. Be sure to connect the characters to the events that happened. Write with passion and enthusiasm. Strengthen and individualise each sentence through your personality and imagination. People might be inspired by the way you write and what you have to say.

Example

After 29 years of marriage I drove up North Rocks Road, Carlingford feeling I was a complete failure as my marriage had ended. In the car I had a few paltry personal possessions. What a mess! I had failed my wife and children, myself, what I believed in, my professional life as a counsellor. I couldn't help myself and I failed God. Tears poured down my cheeks. In the journey to my counselling centre at Lane Cove I had to stop and gain composure.

Summary: Readers are attracted to honest writers. This story brings the character alive as I describe a significant episode of my life which moves the story to the next stage. By staying in the moment long enough it helps the reader to feel the intensity of the experience.

Humour Makes A Powerful Connection

Humour is part of life. People love funny stories and enjoy a good belly laugh. It is integral to social interaction and it has long been postulated that humour may enhance quality of life, assist in stress management, and help us cope with the stresses of life. At times we take life too seriously and write about tragedy and drama only. Humour can be a part of tragedy too. Albert Hubbard said "Don't take life too seriously as you will never come out of it alive". Laughter, like tears, is merely a coping mechanism we use to deal with the tough stuff that comes our way.

You Have Your Own Brand Of Humour

A sense of humour is as unique as a person. Everyone has very different ideas about what is and isn't funny. You may have read or listened to a joke and had a great belly laugh as it sounded hilarious. At a later date you tell the same joke to a group of people and it falls flat.

The same is true for writers. Some people will enjoy a funny story and others may be too overcome with embarrassment or perhaps it sticks too close to home so that the humour is lost on the reader. When humour is introduced you need to decide which direction your story will go. You can build on humour to make a point.

Do you have a favourite joke that friends or family loved or hated? Babies and young children are a great source of humorous memories. Pets too have usually performed in some way that offers opportunity for an amusing anecdote. Celebrations such as Christmas, birthdays and weddings offer great opportunities for laughing and joking and funny happenings.

Example

I had just finished conducting a deeply serious religious wedding ceremony for a couple on an ornamental bridge over a large lily and goldfish pond at a reception centre. It had a sombre rather than a celebratory atmosphere and the guests were unresponsive. The wedding party moved off the bridge to sign the marriage register. I pulled the chair out for the bride to sit down, stepped back straight into the pond – robes and all. The guests roared with laughter when I looked up, knee deep in the water and said "Any baptisms?" It certainly took a great effort to gain a reaction.

Summary: With vivid description, humour can break up a serious story. The story becomes real as it unfolds through story telling elements – the seriousness of the service, my time in the pond with the goldfish, the embarrassment (which is not stated) and the response from the guests. There is good pacing and reader interest as it is an unusual story.

Humour Reveals Another Side To Your Character

Reflect on some of the funny things that have happened to you along the way. Every story in which humour has played a part in your life and health is a story worth telling. Some Eastern philosophers place laughter next to enlightenment. A person who is capable of laughing at oneself has learned an important lesson in life's journey.

Here are some guidelines that will help you add humour to your story:

Short is almost always better than long, be concise and direct.

Simple is almost always better than complex: If the story doesn't seem to be working, try simplifying the presentation and/or words.

Abandon judgment: a statement is often funny because it's illogical.

Abandon your pride: your story can't be funny if you're afraid of embarrassing yourself.

Don't try too hard to be funny. That just makes your humour feel stilted or laboured. Allow it to reflect your style.

Don't sacrifice truth for a funny effect. Humour always contains some truth; without truth, it's just playing with words.

Most importantly - have fun with it yourself. If you enjoy it, chances are your readers will, too.

Comedy Versus Tragedy

It is far easier for most people to write about tragedy than about comedy. Tragic events are often embodied in our mind because of the impact that has been made. Humorous experiences make a lesser impact and are often easily forgotten. A writer with a good sense of humour has a real advantage. They can see instantly the funny side of life and are prepared to laugh at themselves and the way they handle particular situations.

Write About Real People, Places and Experiences

Your readers like to identify with the people, places and experiences you recollect in your story. Think about the times you watched a travelogue or news on television which has shown a place you have visited. You instantly have a heightened awareness and a deep involvement in the story as memories flood into your mind. The same is true about places you describe in your writing.

True to life experiences lift your story from an historical account to a personal level. We live in a world full of reality TV which takes the viewer behind the scenes and gives them a glimpse of the real TV character. This is exactly what happens when we write about personal experiences.

Example

In my time in the Presbyterian Ministry, the Presbytery of North Sydney was known as one of the most difficult. The Presbytery consisted of all Ministers north of the Harbour together with Church Elders. It was a governing and controlling group which ministers needed to report to.

When I applied for permission to go into counselling in the early 1970s, and being the first minister of any denomination to make this transition, I expected a difficult reception. I was armed with documents, letters, facts and supporting papers. To my amazement the Presbytery and its members agreed unanimously to the request. This I believed was a miracle, or maybe it was the way to get rid of me from a parish.

Summary: This story is a good illustration of an anti-climax. I was ready to do battle but there was none. In the example I supplied the facts, provided a description of the Presbytery, and built up some tension in the story. The story then unfolds almost as a "fizzer" except for my last remark that causes the reader to think.

Positive People With Positive Stories

People are attracted to positive people who have made a success of life. They usually have encouraging and optimistic stories to tell. People generally aspire to be successful; there is an expectation that we try to succeed at something. When not taken to the extreme, being successful is an important and positive goal to value, but it can be a frustrating journey. Give your story a positive slant. Convey through your writing that a person with a positive attitude to life can conquer challenging situations.

A Journey Into A Period Of History

Your writing is an opportunity for the reader to take a journey into a period of history, to discover what it was like in bygone days. Was it a period in our history of affluence or poverty, and what were the fashions of the day? What was different about people in these times? What special events and political situations stand out for you? Write about meals and special foods, games, leisure activities, family relationships.

It is a well-established fact that our childhood influences affect the way we react to certain situations today. This will be evident in your writing. Many of your readers will be interested to hear about what life and times were like when you were growing up. Some people think the good old days were better than the present time but in reality this is not always so. We all have a tendency to block out the hurtful past and try to remember the good times. We should also remember there are some people who dwell on the hurtful past and never move on.

The reader may compare their values and beliefs of the past with values of the present. Have we marked time, advanced or lost our way? Through writing we are able to assess our new values and beliefs and to see if they have made us into better people. The reader identifies with changes that have taken place in your life and that of our country.

Example

I have had only one farm holiday and that was on my Uncle Dick's farm at Elimbah near Beerburrum on the Queensland Sunshine Coast. The house was little more than a shack with no electricity or running water. With great excitement I travelled there by steam train with my father and two older cousins. I was nine at the time. At night my cousins would tell ghost stories and I can remember wetting my pants I was so scared.

Uncle Dick grew pineapples as well as peanuts which I thought grew on trees until I discovered they grow under the ground. Learning about pineapples from my uncle helped me later when I was in ministry at nearby Glasshouse Mountains, part of the pineapple growing region.

Summary: My story slowly comes together with descriptions of location, train travel, older cousins, no electricity or running water. The reader is transported to a small outback farm. The scene changes on arrival and the reader finds out about peanuts and pineapples. Uncle Dick remains as a background character.

Love and Romance Make Good Stories

Basically most of us are sentimentalists at heart and love a romantic story. Romance allows you to put passion and excitement into your writing by revealing your tenderness and sensitivity. Take time to recall your early romances and perhaps your awkwardness with the opposite sex, funny experiences, embarrassing moments, captivating and tantalizing encounters. Share experiences that were heartbreaking at the time because to lose someone can be devastating. Be prepared to share your feelings about love and early adulthood and how love was expressed or not, in your home.

Example

I had taken a stunning blond by the name of Joy to a school formal at Cloudland, a popular dance hall in Brisbane. Up to this time I had never kissed a girl as I was too shy. Tonight was to be the night as the hormones were running hot.

We both had a great night at the dance and as I walked her up the garden path the porch light came on and the front door opened and Joy said "Daddy is waiting I must go in". I said goodnight and left bitterly disappointed. It was a short-lived romance.

Summary: The usual story is boy meets girl, they kiss and fall in love. The story of my first kiss was one of sheer disappointment. I laid a strong foundation for the story, revealing what I hoped would happen and the intensity builds as I walk up the path. My writer's voice demonstrates my disappointment when the light comes on and the door opens.

Writing About Sexual Encounters

The more comfortable you are with your sexuality the more freedom you will have to write about sexual experiences. For a part of my professional life I was a sexual therapist and include my own definition of sexuality "sexuality is love of self, love of others, love of life; it is the masculine and feminine in each of us." Our sexuality affects every area of our life – personality, self esteem, self confidence, personal identity. It is not just something we do in bed. Sexuality is life energy force we use in our daily life, based on self love. Sexuality and spirituality go together as both of these experiences take us into another world. The writer needs to be discrete and not turn the story into a pornographic narrative. When writing about these experiences make sure you are the main character and that the privacy of others is protected.

People Who Touched Your Life

Take time to recall some memorable characters that have influenced your life. Some people come into our life for a short period and are soon gone, others become life long friends.

Use your creativity in describing how you met these people and the influence they had on your life. They could be relatives, family, neighbours, teachers, colleagues, sporting heroes etc. Describe their personality and character and why you were attracted to them.

People need not be famous to be memorable. Ordinary people who have influenced your life in some way are often the most unforgettable. Often they have been school teachers although sometimes the meeting may be only for a fleeting moment. Write about the effect that these people had upon your life – good or bad. Tell how the meeting changed your destiny.

Recognising these people through your life story is a way to say thank you. This may not have happened when you were involved with them. If these people have hurt you it is a way of completing unfinished business. Even though many may no longer be alive their memory lingers strong in your life for whatever reason and it is an opportunity to share their impact.

Sharing Values and Beliefs – Things That Matter

All the time we are making discoveries about life. Be prepared to share these discoveries, or your philosophy of life, in a way that makes a meaningful connection with your reader.

A person's way of life is based upon a personal philosophy. Knowing this helps the reader to see how a person thinks, what they deem important and significant in their life and how they respect themselves and others. Values and beliefs are revealed through actions and reactions. Readers recognize what is good for one person is not always good for another. We can understand a lot more about a person through their living environment, personality, educational achievement, age, health and other experiences through their writing.

WRITING EXERCISE FOR LESSON EIGHT

1. Read through your first rough draft and make a list of the stories you have included.

2. Take time to rethink chapter headings. Try naming chapters which arouse reader curiosity. Think about humorous chapter headings.

3. Now it is time to reassemble your material and to see where the various stories could make a better impact. It is time to be experimental.

Writing Your Life Story With Creativity and Imagination

*"It doesn't matter how slowly you
go, so long as you do not stop."*

- Confucius

Writing Creatively – Ignite The Imagination

Creativity is not limited to great artists, poets, writers, inventors, sculptors or film makers. It exists deep within us and is waiting to be released. We need to let go of that old script "I am not creative". If we live out this script it is a sure way to block any creative expression. Unleash your creativity by returning to your childhood world of play in the "land of make believe". A creative person is like a child curious, experimental, adventurous and playful.

Inspired flourishes lift our story as we create word pictures. Imaginative and resourceful people use their awareness to see things in a different way. Thoughts and ideas are visualised in the mind and then transferred to the page. Allow time for incubation of the idea as it becomes clear in your thinking.

Example

In the early 1970s I regularly visited Dangar Island and told my friends "I am going down the Hawkesbury River on the QE2". I travelled from Brooklyn on the Hawkesbury to Dangar on the small ferry. Once on Dangar Island I would board my version of the QE2, which was a small boatshed on a jetty with the water flowing underneath.

A well-to-do friend wanted to come down with his children and share the experience. This man had never camped and had always stayed in 5 star hotels. I did not tell him there were no showers, poor toilet facilities and only camp beds to sleep on. My own children were sworn to secrecy. We arrived on the island at 9pm and had to walk with torchlight on a narrow track half way around the island to reach our destination. On arrival not a word was spoken, his face said everything. However at the end of the weekend he knew something of what I experienced, but he never came again.

Summary: I use imagination to build the story and description of my QE2 liner. I release my inner child as I deal with the request from my well-to-do friend. The story ends with a partial anticlimax and also an experience I am sure he will never forget.

Writing Playfully – Release Your Inner Child

As a life storywriter believe there is a fun side to your nature. It is a well-established psychological fact that the "inner child", our playful side, often does not come through clearly to our family and friends. Here is an opportunity to play a little and share fun experiences and perhaps enjoy your "second childhood". Play, dream, have fun and build castles in the air to stir your imagination.

Example

A scruffy looking stray dog found its way into the Rainworth State School grounds and at lunchtime I would feed it the crusts from my sandwiches. One day, to my "surprise", the dog followed me home. I named him Socks and Dad thought he was a nice dog and helped me to persuade Mum to keep him, which wasn't easy as we already had Tinker the cat.

Two weeks later there was a pets' parade at Moorlands at Milton Riach on the Brisbane River. Socks won two prizes "The Best Mongrel" and "The Best Boy's Companion". I received a cup, a torch and a ribbon. The cup and the ribbon sat on my wardrobe for years. Socks soon became a loved member of our family and truly a boy's best friend.

Summary: My story moves the reader as a stray dog finds a loving home. I am writing playfully as I feed the dog at school and then bring it home. I also use words to describe the conflict in getting the dog accepted by my parents. The story ignites with Socks winning prizes at the Pets' Parade and comes home as a hero with his tail wagging.

Writing Visually – Be an Artist With Words

Think of your writing as a drive into the country where the scenery is continually changing. At times a country drive can be uninteresting but other times the scenery can be delightful. Vary your writing style to suit the mood of your story. Paint pictures with words to grab the reader's attention.

You know what you want to say but you are looking for a different way to express your thoughts. People are attracted to those who are flamboyant and stand out in a crowd. Others feel threatened by these personalities. To be creative with words you need to convey your spectrum of emotions and produce them in a way that makes the reader think. Draw attention to issues that you feel are important and worthy of consideration.

Use Creativity, Imagination And Playfulness To Produce Aliveness

Readers love colourful individuals. If your life has been colourful help it to shine through the pages. Bring alive your manuscript by revealing all sides of your nature – the fun and the serious side.

Write about the playful and entertaining side of your nature. Describe the way you play and have fun along the pathway of life by building that into your story. It does not matter how remarkable or out of the ordinary these events may appear. They add colour and excitement as humour can help lighten your story. This encourages the reader to laugh with you and gain a glimpse of your humanity.

Writing Spontaneously – Play Your Hunches, Listen To Your Intuition

Are you a writer who thinks outside the square and is prepared to take some risks by playing your hunches and listening to your intuition? This approach will add a new dimension to your writing. The more you believe in yourself the more ready you will be to run these calculated risks. Some of these ideas will not lead anywhere, but they are worth exploring.

Example

On our trip around Australia we came to a sign that pointed to Onslow which was 70kms off the main highway on the West Australian coast. We decided to call in and explore the small fishing town. It was the right decision!

We stayed at a motel on the beachfront. Carmel was standing at the kitchen window looking out to the ocean as the motel manager walked past carrying a large painted lobster, fresh out of the water. She was straight out the door to admire it and without hesitation the manager, Sue, asked if we would like it. "Graham would love it" Carmel said. I went down to the water's edge with my bucket to collect salt water in which to cook the lobster while Carmel chatted with Sue. She surprised us further with some beautiful mackerel fillets. There is a regular guest to the motel, a prawn fisherman, who pays his bill with prawns. So when we came to check out of the motel the next morning we left with a big bag of fresh prawns as well. We were so pleased we took the road to Onslow.

Summary: It is evident that we played a hunch to visit Onslow which paid off handsomely. A road taken or not taken usually applies to life changing decisions, but this story demonstrates how a gut feeling took us to something totally unexpected and showed how kind and generous people can be. It remains in our memory as a very special time and place.

Colour Your World With Sensory Perception

Our senses help to define our world and the way we experience it. They help us to visualise a person doing something so the setting and the image of the person becomes real. Explore the senses and see how they can be included in your writing experience.

Sight: Help the reader to see characteristics they have never noticed previously. Most people are visual. Television and the movie screen has been a major influence. Create a picture with your character or scene in action.

Sound: Add life to your writing by introducing sounds – the sound of the wind between the trees, the noise of thunder during a storm, the sound of gunfire, the flow of water across the rocks, the crackling noise from the loudspeaker.

Consider too the sound of stillness or silence that can often be experienced – not a sound in the whole house, the calm before the storm, a town at dawn, high on a mountain, out in a desert.

Taste: If writing about food, describe how it tastes and describe the sheer enjoyment as you share this fabulous or not so fabulous fare. How does this food affect you and what is the mood it produces within you?

Smell: A beautiful smell of freshly cooked bread makes one hungry. A person walks by wearing an appealing perfume that causes heads to turn and look. Create a scene through your writing to help the reader identify with a smell related to the experience you are describing. You may be writing about a seaside experience so create the smell of a salty sea breeze gently blowing across the sand and transport the reader directly to the beach.

Touch: This is one of the most neglected areas of writing. We sometimes have an inbuilt fear of touch. If we accidentally touch someone we instantly apologise as we feel we are invading his or her space. Surely the aim of the writer is to touch the life of the reader in some way. We touch our readers emotionally by sharing our honesty through the experiences that have made an impact upon us. They can be humorous, embarrassing or moments of true elation.

Sensory observation is a potent skill to use in order to convey your message.

Example

For two hours I enjoyed massage to music by two therapists working in unison. It was a new massage therapy developed by Kay Ortman in America called Relax & Rebound. Classical music was playing while the therapists worked on my body. When the music was soft the movement of the hands would be gentle. The massage would be stronger and more in depth when the music picked up. At the end of the massage I felt 10 years younger, alive and alert. Kay wanted me to experience the process and bring the program to Australia supported by these two therapists. I missed a golden opportunity because I declined the offer.

Summary: The reader becomes involved in the story by this unusual approach to massage therapy. The facts that are needed to build the story are there in detail. The story is captivating as there is a gentle build-up of the sensual. As a storyteller my enthusiasm for the program is revealed by the benefits I experienced. Then there is a deep regret that I missed the opportunity to bring the program to Australia.

The Surprise Factor – Roads Taken/Not Taken

Recall the roads in your life taken and not taken. Surprise your reader with unexpected twists and turns, of imagination, adventure and excitement. What will happen next? You have your reader excited and wanting to turn the next page. Life's "what ifs" make for good reading. Opportunities missed can teach us valuable lessons.

Developing Your Colourful Characters

The best way to kill a life story is to write a narrative full of historical events and people without reflecting on how they have influenced you, or moved you emotionally. It is not always facts and information that people want, but an insight into the real nature of the individual. Think about some of the characters you have met, any eccentricities about them, mannerisms, dress code, typical sayings, or strong opinions? Perhaps one or more of your characters is a loveable rogue. Write in a way that is non-judgemental of these characters but helps to bring them alive. Give your reader an opportunity to get to know them. Colourful characters make a lasting impression upon the reader.

Example

As a young teenager of 15 I thought Auntie Dell was a colourful individual in her own right. She was manageress of Allan & Stark Restaurant and Cake Shop (now Myers). She always dressed in colourful, stylish outfits, and wore a rich red lipstick. She was plump and cheerful, somewhat bossy with staff, but she utterly spoilt me. I often had afternoon tea with her when I was attending high school. She loved to drink and go to the races with her boyfriend Ken. She smoked and I thought she was a with-it lady. Unfortunately she died at 42 from kidney failure. My world collapsed for she played a very special part in my life.

Summary: I tried to develop this colourful character through the eyes of a 15 year old. I have tried to capture the attention of the reader by her compelling character and her freedom to be herself. Sadness is introduced by her untimely death.

Characters Have a Magical Quality

This magical quality is best described as something that sets them apart from other people. I like to think of it in the form of one's own uniqueness. This magical quality ensures that the character makes an impact upon the reader. Most people have magical qualities but it is more developed in some than in others.

Turning Ordinary Events Into Extraordinary Events

A writer can turn an ordinary event into an extraordinary event using the right words. For example at a dinner party a guest transforms the gathering into something very special by their personality or the discussion around the table or it is perhaps the unusual or extraordinary menu provided by the host or way of decorating the table. This helps to turn an ordinary party into a special event, through a little imaginative expression whilst keeping to the essence of the story.

Example

Two weeks after my arrival at John Knox Church in Rockhampton I met the church cleaner, Daisy Laurence. This good lady cared for her mother until she died. Now at 69 years of age Daisy lived off a small pension and her income from cleaning the church. Even though she had little, this poor lady gave back the wages she earned by her cleaning as her offering to God every Sunday.

Daisy had no close friends, she became a part of our family and when our children John and Ruth arrived she became surrogate Grandmother and baby sitter. Towards the end of our six years in Rockhampton I was able to get Daisy into a church retirement settlement where she had a brand new home – small but comfortable. She stayed there until she died ten years later. She was a true saint of God.

Summary: I have taken an ordinary person and turned her into an extraordinary person – a true saint of God. I have hooked the reader to feel a little sad for Daisy and then supplied sufficient information to describe her poverty. I have used motivation and action to provide a happy ending.

Use Creativity And Imagination When You Entertain

People want to be entertained as they read. They become conditioned to entertainment through involvement with television and other media. Entertaining stories come to us unexpectedly. Steven Spielberg claims his best story ideas come to him when he is driving.

Embarrassing experiences that happen to us later become entertaining stories. It shows we are prepared to laugh at ourselves and rise above the situation. A writer can generate a sense of suspense in the readers mind as he relates an embarrassing situation, especially if it has an unlikely twist.

WRITING EXERCISES FOR LESSON NINE

1. Write about an experience that is vivid in your mind. Use your creativity, imagination and originality to develop your theme. Notice how it brings your story alive.

2. Now rewrite your first draft using this technique of creativity and imagination to lift your writing to a new level. Do not be afraid to use humorous headings for paragraphs or chapters. You are now adding aliveness and colour to your writing experience.

3. Think of a creative title for your life story. Do a rough cover design and then employ the services of a graphic artist if you wish.

Taking Your Life Story To A Deeper Level

*"Everyone has talent. What is rare is
the courage to follow that talent to
the dark place where it leads."*

- Erica Jong

Delving Deeper – Making Your Life Story More Meaningful

In life we typically play it safe and keep our discussions at a shallow level. Writing superficially about people or events is easy. Delving deeper into how they felt or how they influenced others' lives takes courage. While writing your story you will be challenged to face some awkward situations. Life's ambiguities, uncertainties and variations are being revisited. Share experiences, places and people who have helped or hurt you in your journey. There is no easy way to handle these situations especially if you are writing about someone else's misfortune. As you look back you may see how you could have handled some of the situations much better. Life is a learning experience.

There are no simple rules that apply. All you can do is to write honestly from your point of view. You need to keep asking yourself "is this incident necessary for my story or could it be omitted?" Maybe if you are finding it so difficult it should not be there in the first place.

Say Things Others Are Afraid To Say

Try to be bold as a writer and really express what you think and feel. Many will admire that you have the guts to say the things others thought but were afraid to say. Be a writer who is prepared to bring issues out into the open for debate. This is being courageous as a writer and shows you are prepared to be honest with issues that are of deep concern. Do not be dogmatic in what you say. Be open to other points of view.

Personal Censorship – What To Put In/Leave Out

You alone know what is necessary and what is not. There are no simple guidelines. This skill comes though experience, commonsense, a feeling of fairness and finally the sobering thought that you could be sued. Some experiences need to be told to make your life story authentic.

Example

I attended a Gestalt therapy (body therapy) workshop conducted at Sydney University by world-renowned therapist Eric Marcus. There were 100 present and I was selected by lucky number to be the morning "guinea pig".

His opening remarks to me as I went up to him were "Graham you are very angry". I almost shouted "No I am not – you've got that wrong". My body language, posture and tone of voice were a give-away. For two hours Eric worked with me and I swore freely in public. I was partly ashamed of the filth that came out of my mouth. I was angry with myself, my mother, my life, God, nearly anyone you could think of. At the end I felt drained but I had got rid of much bottled up anger. For the rest of the day I was spaced out and cared for by a group of therapists.

Summary: The scene quickly evolves – what my story is about, where it is, some insight into the leader and issues in my life needing attention are addressed. The language soon creates the mood for the story. At times there is dramatic dialogue. Powerful words are used to express the way I feel.

Censorship – Know Where To Stop

Analyse why you feel you need to include this experience in your story. Think about it. Would it be wiser to use it, or leave it out? This is a question you need to face honestly. If it relates to your life it is a much easier decision to make. If it relates to someone else, the decision is harder. A good rule of thumb for a writer is when in doubt, leave it out.

Protect Family Secrets

Be responsible as a writer. Learn to write with honesty and sensitivity. Use common sense in order to protect the privacy of members of your family. Say what needs to be said to move your story forward without hurting other members.

Do Not Gloss Over Awkward Situations

At times you may not be 100% sure of your facts but do not bluff your way through. Be honest and say that your knowledge is sketchy. Your thoughts may be jumbled and you may need to crystallise your thinking. Do not run away from the unimpressive side of your life by trying to cover it up. Let it all hang out that it is important in your story. Many of your readers will know you fairly well and soon spot flaws in your story. Do not misrepresent the facts.

Accepting Personal Responsibility – Not Blaming Others

As you write about the events of your life, make it abundantly clear that you take full responsibility for the way you acted. This reveals a state of maturity in your life. Life strikes some mean blows which we are unable to answer in simple human terms. Good fortune and misfortune are a part of life. Sometimes we happen to be in the right place at the right time or the wrong place at the wrong time.

You see each experience of life as a learning experience. Blaming someone else for your disappointments achieves very little. Rise above life's problems.

Writing About Your True Self

We often go through life playing pretend games and no one really knows the real person. We become experts and live out a lie. Be daring and reveal yourself. It's time to let readers see your fears, insecurities, as well as successes and satisfying projects. If you are not being yourself it is a waste of time writing your life story. You gain reader empathy through your honesty as you share your hurts, resentments and regrets.

Example

As a child I grew up thinking to be accepted I needed to be polite, nice and not upset anyone. I lived like this until I was 50. I wore an imaginary sign around my neck "Please kick me – I won't kick back". In the ministry I was a failure as I kept turning the other cheek. I believe one of the main reasons I took up counselling was to find myself. Counselling helped me to find my identity which many did not like as I was no longer the nice guy, but rather the honest guy.

Summary: There is a sense of movement in my story as I search to find myself. I am willing as a writer to push and explore boundaries and belief. My journey of discovery is based on honesty and openness.

Breaking Open Your Psychological Shell

For a reader to get to know you there is need to break open your psychological shell. Do this by stepping out of your comfort zone. Sometimes, we go through life playing games and hiding behind a psychological façade. Times of discontent, pain and frustration are hidden. Focus on any change the experiences brought to your life and the way you responded.

Example

Whilst studying in the United States I met Lucille Ball's aunt who obtained tickets for me to go with Lucille's mother to the recording of the "I Love Lucy Show". I went to dinner with Lucy's elderly eccentric mother who introduced me to horseradish with which I proceeded to cover my steak. We had a lovely meal even with tears streaming down my cheeks.

At the "warm up" before the show commenced I was invited on stage to meet Lucy. It was the final of the series and I was also invited to a celebration party at her home. On her arrival she sought me out and took me for a tour of her lovely home. At this time she was in crises and needed to talk to someone. At this meeting I saw Lucy's serious side but once we returned to the guests her voice changed and her stage personality reappeared.

Summary: I have used this story to captivate the emotional life of the character – the humorous and the serious. I break up the story with my folly with the horseradish. Most of my readers will know she is a comic actor so I do not go into too much detail. The story moves on the page with Lucy's need to talk about the crises. The aim of the story is to reveal the character and what she is really like away from her TV image.

Meaningful Incidents That Have Changed Your Life

What important events in your life have become major turning points? Perhaps an illness that caused you to make a major decision. Have you invented a gadget, heard a significant address, read a meaningful book, or suffered the loss of someone close to you? Has (early) retirement, starting up your own business or a magical moment when you responded to an idea had a major bearing on your life? Discuss the battles and how you overcame them. Show how these incidents really made an impact upon your life and changed your direction.

Example

The New Age movement made me realise that the Christian Church has no ownership of God. When I met Carmel she belonged to a healing spiritualist group. When

I attended my first meeting with her I was sure God would strike me down and punish me for going to such a meeting. I was mighty scared. Here I met a group of people who were on a spiritual journey although there was little mention of God. I attended a number of these meetings and I felt blessed. This experience broadened my view of God. I am sure that not many other ministers would have shared this type of experience.

Summary: Here I share one of life's experiences which ends up broadening my view of spirituality. The story describes my fears. There is rigid judgmental thought not experienced that God belongs to the church. As the story and sequence evolves I acknowledge that I was blessed in some way. At the end of the story I make a dramatic statement which is left unexplained that the experience broadened my view of God.

Conflicts Are a Part Of Life

Conflicts help us to grow as individuals. These are all around us in family, at work, and amongst our friends. They can be of major importance or minor when someone differs from our point of view.

Take time to recall some major conflicts when you felt your personal integrity was being threatened. Perhaps when you were called up for war service there was a conflict between your loyalty to country and your own personal conviction that war was wrong. You could decide to write about a family conflict that has never been resolved.

Whatever the conflict, be prepared to write in a way that depicts how you felt at the time and with introspection how it could have been resolved more amicably.

Example

At high school the boys sat around and bragged about their so-called "exploits" with girls they met at school or other places. I did my part in the bragging parade. Oh! What an imagination I had.

The subject of war was a common discussion point. At this time World War II was taking place. The boys boasted freely about enlisting, going to war and picking up chicks in every city and seeing the world for free. I disagreed with the discussion as I had an inner conflict based on biblical injunction "Thou shalt not kill". I was a pacifist and thought war was senseless. The only problem was I was too weak to express my convictions.

Summary: This is a good example of inner conflict and acceptance at any price. Facts are sketchy. I hide in the story and do not reveal my real thoughts in my peer group for fear of rejection. I structure the story to include bragging, big time, to contrast with the real person. My story plot evolves as facts are slowly revealed. The story is told to inspire, instruct and inform readers of options available.

Writing With Honesty and Clarity

When writing about yourself do so without exaggerating all your characteristics. Do not censor essential information about yourself, but try to be transparent so that readers can see the real you.

Do not give anyone reason to attack your writing. No one can prevent anyone reading his or her own thoughts into your story and drawing the wrong conclusion. You are responsible to present your material so clearly that it cannot be misinterpreted. There will be some people who will disagree with you in some events you describe but accept it and do not let it upset you.

Nothing clarifies better than writing. When you mull things over in your mind you often go around in circles and get nowhere. By writing down your thoughts they become clearer and a structure begins to form. This offers you a framework on which to build. You will let go of some thoughts and re-examine others.

As you do this you will be amazed at what you stumble upon. It could be a moment of inspiration which makes a marked impression and helps you to gain valuable awareness. Be prepared to experiment and to take some calculated risks in the stories you tell. Use your commonsense to censor material that sounds confusing or not necessary. Know what to throw away and what to keep in your story by asking the question "Is this material essential in moving my story forward?"

Write With Sensitivity – Respect Of Self And Others

Writers need to be truthful without being spiteful or vindictive. Never write something that you may regret. Consider others' feelings. Be sensitive to the reader reaction to your characters and what you have to say about them. Some people want to defend others when the facts appear to be distorted from their perspective. There is a way to tell the truth without destroying the individual.

Sharing Your Success Without Bragging

In writing about your accomplishments it is important to talk about what life was like, the state of the nation, family loyalty, fashion trends, value of money and much more. The occupation you followed may no longer exist. Describe items your company perhaps made by hand that are now made by machine. Discuss the wages and conditions and perhaps your work ethic. Our world has changed so rapidly and this could make interesting reading.

Speak about your career development including progress and setbacks. This is good for you to reflect upon and see what you have achieved. As you look at life you will notice a pattern evolving which not only helps you to review your career but it also says much about who you are as a person.

If you were in a leadership role show how you handled situations. Think about the positions you held at different times in your life and how you felt about them e.g. work, homemaker, volunteer etc.

Satisfying Community Projects

Recall any satisfying community projects in which you have participated. Think about service clubs, sporting organisations, church groups, political parties, environmental and cultural activities etc. Take time to write about what you did and the satisfaction you received. Some people find community projects more satisfying than their paid employment.

Difficulties and Disappointments

Certainly it is often easier to write about nice things that happen in your life, but bear in mind it is meaningful for the reader to share in your difficulties and how you handled the tough situation of life. These challenging parts animate your story. Although you might present a condensed version of your difficulties with less emotional charge, you recognise that this is an important experience to share.

By writing about your fears, challenges, erroneous beliefs, false assumptions you start to build your self-confidence. For some it feels like a weight lifted off your shoulders. Instead of hiding your fears and anxieties you acknowledge them and bring them out into the open.

Example

At primary school I was a poor student especially when it came to maths and I rarely passed a maths test. I sat for the State Scholarship Examination (Year 8) which gave entry into high school. With fear and trepidation I opened the Courier Mail in Brisbane where the results were first published by a newspaper. Yes, I had failed. I felt like a dunce sitting in the corner wearing a dunce's cap.

All the other children in the street passed the examination. For a week I felt terrible and people did not know what to say. Auntie Dell came to my rescue after I received the results. I passed all subjects but maths.

Auntie Dell paid my fees to high school where I attended State Commercial High School which had been only for girls until 1944. That year I enrolled in English, history, bookkeeping, commerce, shorthand/typing and maths. The school had 1200 girls and 100 boys. I thought I had struck it lucky. "Farmer Jones" the maths teacher took an interest in me and gave me extra work. My life took off and I passed the junior examination two years later and won the school prize for English expression. My social life was also tops.

Summary: I share openly my disappointment with the examination results. My feelings are clearly described, also the reaction of the neighbours. In the story Auntie Dell and the friendly maths teacher "Farmer Jones" rescue me. I turn my failure and disappointment into success by passing the junior examination and winning the English expression prize.

Painful Moments – Significant Decisions

We put off making painful decisions because we don't want to hurt others or ourselves. Eventually life forces us to make a decision. Life's disappointments and painful decisions may slow us down but do not stop us from moving ahead.

Write about the way you felt when you had to make a painful decision forced upon you when conditions were out of your control. Perhaps you were forced to make staff redundant because of company reorganisation. Another scenario could be the loss of your home through financial problems not necessarily from your making.

A painful moment could be the loss of a loved one in a tragic accident. Often painful moments happen unexpectedly.

Other times we procrastinate from making a painful decision hoping the problem will go away. It could be a decision to end a marriage as we do not want to hurt ourselves and others.

Share the internal battle which preceded the painful decision. Discuss the ways you recovered from this and significant decisions you made as you faced your future.

Unlived Hopes – Missed Opportunities

Here is an opportunity to share unfulfilled dreams and missed opportunities. It was Oliver Wendell Holmes who said "The great thing about life is not where we are but in what direction we are moving".

Share your frustrations about unfulfilled dreams, the pain and the sadness of this and your hope for the future.

If you have some regrets about missed opportunities write about why you were afraid to follow them or why you failed to recognise them when they came your way.

Clearing Clutter – Healing/Therapeutic Writing

Our lives are frequently cluttered with unfinished business from the past. This sometimes does not allow us to move onto the present. Writing your life story is a way to remove emotional and physical clutter. It is a way to work through emotional disappointments from the past and discharge them from your life.

Writing about these experiences can be healing and therapeutic. When they are brought out into the open, aired, and addressed and thoughts recorded there is a sense of completion. By writing honestly you are able to accept responsibility for past mistakes. If the experience is an "act of God" and defies human explanation, all you can do is to accept it and move forward e.g. loss of a child through illness. This is a valuable piece of writing your life story and can give you a new sense of personal freedom by letting go of the past.

How Much Of Your Life And Experiences Do You Reveal?

It can be a real struggle to decide what to put into your story and what to leave out. Take time for positive convincing and introspection into your life. Make a list of experiences that have deeply affected your life. Decide on the best approach for you to protect others.

To decide what to write ask these two questions:

1. What am I ready to reveal?

2. How significant will this information be in the development of my life story?

In your personal journal record everything. In your work for publication, edit some sensitive material which may provoke controversy and achieve very little.

You will have to fight your way through the wilderness of confusion before you decide what is important and what is not. Keep asking the questions "Should I cut this out?" Another question to be considered: "Is this part of my life of interest only to me and not to the reader?" It may not be until the second or third draft before you know if it is relevant.

Things I Have Never Told You

This might be a suitable chapter title to take your story to a deeper level as you share some of the upheavals and disappointments in your life. For whatever reason there may have been stories from your past you have never shared. Now you are prepared to share these secrets. These stories need not be big dark secrets but little or fun things that have not been told, or an experience out of character.

Example

I went to a body, mind and spirit seminar in the Gold Coast hinterland attended by about 500. Most of the people were naked. I wanted to run away and go home. Laurie Cambridge, my mentor, was with me and told me I needed to face this challenge. I was extremely uncomfortable and went for a walk by myself along the creek where I met a young woman who shared with me her background in psychology and she helped me to see myself.

After some contemplation I decided to join the crowd "au naturale" and enjoyed a new found freedom. There was something very liberating about the experience but I never did it again.

Summary: This story is out of character for me and I have used it as a way to plant seeds to bear some fruit later in my story. It is a way to reminisce and to appreciate each step of my journey. It introduces a change of scene. The interaction with the psychologist helps to develop story sequence.

Valuable Information From Your Personal Journal

From your personal journal writings you will likely find a wealth of information which will take your story to a deeper level. This can be a period of genuine enlightenment as you have used thoughts and words describing essential details of events which make for good stories.

WRITING EXERCISES FOR LESSON TEN

1. Go back over rough draft number two and check for honesty, clarity and sensitivity.

2. Now go back and rewrite sections in your story that lack clarity of expression. Make sure you clearly present all the facts and do not try and embellish them.

3. Take time to look for stories that could be omitted that do not add to your story. Rethink embarrassing situations especially if they affect others.

Now is the time to make your story more meaningful and to record experiences that have made a significant impact upon your life. These stories may be related to painful events or successful achievements.

Page Fright – Overcoming Writers' Block

"Love your material. Nothing frightens the inner critic more than the writer who loves his/her work."

- Allegra Goodman

You Are Blocked – A Common Complaint

At times our thoughts become muddled, we lose a sense of direction and our mind becomes a blank. We stare at a piece of paper and nothing happens. You want to write but you can't. Or you can only write rubbish. The technical term is "writer's block". Writer's block happens for several reasons, but it could simply be physical or emotional tiredness. Writing requires a sacrifice of time and energy and we may feel lethargic, empty, not wanting to be there or not in the mood to do anything. Recognise it as a temporary setback and that it will pass.

No Tricks To Overcome Writers' Block

Most authors find writer's block causes them to revaluate what they have written. It happens when we least expect it. The body, mind and brain are telling us that its time to take a break. Do not give up on your project, but put a sign on the door - "Gone Fishing". You need to go and play some sport, go out for lunch, go to a movie or simply have a good rest and read a book. Do something that is simply for fun.

Setting Standards Too High

By setting too high a standard you could feel disappointed and want to give up on the project. You could feel blocked and unable to proceed. Keep remembering there is no such thing as the perfect manuscript. Set your standards high by all means, but do not be disheartened if you don't quite get there. It is important not to compare yourself with others. People want to see you through your writing not your technical expertise.

Your Readership May Worry You

Whether it's feedback we've asked for or an unsolicited remark, criticism and rejection are a huge part of our lives. Sometimes we're so fearful of being criticised we have difficulty in expressing exactly what we want to say or we censor vital information because of our concern of what others might think. In your writing you may be hoping for a specific reaction or response. Keep your end goal in mind, the reason for writing your story or a particular part of your story. Remember that your sense of self-worth comes from inside of you. When you're able to be confident in yourself regardless of the feedback you get from external sources, or what you think you might get, you're able to bounce back much more easily from any negative feedback that you may get. Focus your attention on the positive and you'll attract more of it.

Conflict In Thoughts

A writer may feel blocked because of conflict in the thought stream. You may be writing at a safe level and perhaps feel the need to go deeper. At this time there is an inner confusion and you may feel blocked as a writer not knowing which way to go. Take time out from writing and in your jottings journal do the following exercise. Divide you page up in two sections "for and against" and keep asking yourself should I go deeper. This exercise will help you to discover which way to go and free you up from your writing block.

Be Self Motivated

Discouragement and lack of motivation hits everyone at some time or another. Usually there is no one around to motivate you. A writer can obtain support from a writers' group but when alone with your thoughts you sometimes feel you have to push yourself to continue. That sort of self-discipline can be self-defeating and a "negative influence".

Instead use positive motivators that will help you eliminate procrastination, boost your productivity, and generally enhance your writing.

Write down your motivation for writing your life story. Set goals within goals. Don't take on the entire project at once. Break it up into manageable sections by giving yourself reasonable goals of a certain number of words or pages to be completed within a certain time frame. After you reach each goal, assign yourself a new one. This step-by-step method will make the project less imposing. If you wear yourself out trying to reach your goal, reassess it.

Constant pushing leads to frustration, and your work isn't as good as it might be under this kind of pressure. Schedule your writing for your best time of day. Stop writing before you grow tired of working at it. Driving yourself too much you'll be reluctant to return to it later. Have some fun. Reward yourself. Give yourself rewards after completing difficult or lengthy parts of your project. Buy yourself a book, take a trip, or go to a movie - whatever constitutes a reward for you.

Free Writing As A Way To Overcome Writer's Block

Free writing is a useful and simple exercise for when you are having difficulties progressing in your writing. Basically you write non-stop for a set period of time. Five to ten minutes is a good guide – set a timer. Write whatever comes into your mind, and keep writing even if you have to write "I'm stuck" or something like that. Ignore punctuation and sentence structure. Do not judge or censor your writing. You can't fail in free writing.

Free writing has several benefits. It can help to release inner tensions that prevent you from writing. It helps you to sidestep the critic within who tells you that you cannot write. It can also help you discover new things to write about. Free writing as a warm up exercise can help you to write spontaneously, play with words, experiment with style and listen to your intuition.

Writing Need Not Be A Solitary Experience

Writing can be a solitary experience, and many prefer it that way. However, associating with other writers has the benefit of sharing your concerns about the writing process and see how others cope. Organise a group of people wishing to write their own life story and agree to meet on a weekly basis. This offers friendship and an opportunity for constructive criticism when work is shared.

Another benefit is that it helps the writer to have a weekly goal to work towards.

Creating Something From Nothing

You start with nothing – a blank page. Now you are about to create something. You have ideas in your head and it is possible you may have a rough outline. There is a vague blueprint in your mind that relates to the structure of your story.

You are the master architect of your story so feel the thrill of creating something from nothing. It is a sense of accomplishment to write a piece of prose that makes sense. The creative spirit stirs you on to keep writing and pages that were once blank are now filled with a meaningful description of your life.

Silencing The Inner Critic

Once and for all be prepared to silence the inner critic. Be proud of what you have already written. You have done much more than many of your friends who are still going to write their life story.

You know deep within yourself why you are investing time and effort in writing your life story. Having this conviction will do much to silence the inner critic.

Some stumbling blocks that need to be faced in order to silence the inner critic:

> **Will I be understood?** Every writer runs this risk. If you write with clarity and honesty about successes and failures you present a balanced viewpoint which helps the reader to understand what you are mean.

> **Will it be good enough?** If you are a perfectionist, this may be a major issue. Authors will tell you that every book could be improved upon. The perfect book does not exist.

You may need to rewrite where necessary if an advisor suggests it. If still unsure, a professional editor's opinion is worthwhile.

Will I have enough material to write about? You will never know until you start to write. The power of recall is amazing. There are so many wonderful things that define a person's life and make for interesting reading. Some have to be precise in their thinking before they write. Allow the book to evolve.

Will others think I am bragging? Yes, some will think this because they are jealous of what you have achieved. Others will be inspired and encouraged by your struggles and honesty. Your effort may encourage others to write their life story. Remember it is not what you say but how you say it which determines reader reaction.

Will my writing demons destroy me? What if my story is not totally accurate? Will my writing separate me from my family? Do I believe that I am capable enough to portray my life? How will I feel if this project is a flop?

Page After Page

By writing one page a day it is possible to write 100 pages in 100 days. Once you pick up momentum as a writer you may find you may produce 120 or more in this period.

For many writers a hundred pages is sufficient for your life story. This work could be completed in three months and with rewriting and editing it could be ready for publication within six months.

Be Your Own Writing Coach As A Way Of Avoiding Writer's Block

At times coaching yourself can be a struggle. Get your goals down on paper and look forward to working your way through them. Sometimes you may find it impossible to squeeze out a coherent paragraph or shape an idea. Boredom, loneliness and even despair start to settle in and you want to give up.

Here are a few positive suggestions to be your own writing coach:

> Break down your writing problems into digestible, achievable chunks.
>
> Notice where your story starts to ramble. Learn to stick to the point under discussion.
>
> If you feel that your style is not really expressive of you, learn to write in a way that reveals you.
>
> Recognise poor writing and be prepared to rewrite with clarity and aliveness.
>
> Recognise good expression and acknowledge it to yourself. Give yourself a pat on the back for a job well done.
>
> Test your story to see if the reader is gripped by your content. Get opinions from others.

Your Writing and Your Moods

Moods are more evident in some people than others. Writers are no exception. Out of my experience with imaginative and creative people I find many to be plagued with this problem. Accept there will be periods in your life when you feel nothing. On other occasions you will feel very much alive, full of energy and words seem to flow freely.

After you have written about a tough time in your life you could feel tired, drained and listless. Allow for recovery time before you continue to write. Everybody will have good and bad days. Recognise these when they come but do not let them stop you from writing. That "inner critic" can get to you at times like these. Accept the fact that these times will pass and do not be too hard on yourself.

Example

During my theological training I met Bill Mills and we became best friends. He was an army chaplain in Vietnam and truly a very godly man. He came back to Australia with leukaemia. The church prayed, anointed him with oil and followed all the scriptural injunctions, but Bill died.

As I marched down Pennant Hills Road behind the carriage carrying his body I had a fight with God. I felt I was the only one out of step in the parade. At that time I wanted to throw away Christianity as I did not think God was a loving man. The battle lasted for a month until I realised God was bigger than Graham Ascough and I had to trust and accept the umpire's decision.

Summary: I have selected my point of view and written a story around it. My anger and frustration with God is very evident. My negative emotions are freely described. I have used realism to capture the hearts and minds of the readers.

WRITING EXERCISES FOR LESSON ELEVEN

1. If page fright hits you simply sit down with your pen or blank computer screen and write about anything that comes into your mind.

2. Make a list of five people who may read your book and try to write about their reaction in a positive manner.

3. Write freely about a real or imagined fear that you have at this time that relates to writing your life story. It even may have been with you right from the beginning.

Editing – Preparing Your Manuscript For Publication

*"Not that the story needs to be long, but it takes
a long while to make it short."*

- Henry Thoreau

Self Editing Is Extremely Difficult

It does not matter how hard you try it is extremely difficult to successfully edit your own manuscript. You cannot be objective as you are not only too emotionally involved, but it is so familiar to you can miss even glaring errors. You need someone with skills in this area that can offer professional tips to improve your text. If you use a professional editor be sure and obtain a quote.

If you cannot afford an editor think of someone who you respect and would tackle the task in a professional manner. This person needs to have a fairly reasonable idea of grammatical construction, honest to point out weaknesses in your story and to apply a constructive criticism approach to your writing.

The Benefits Of An Editor

Be prepared to have an honest critique made of your own work. An editor helps to polish your work to make it more readable. The editor can spot weaknesses in your manuscript and suggest solutions. Sometimes you may be stuck and do not know how to proceed. A good editor will reduce your wordage. So often we use ten words when two or three will serve the same purpose. It is a great gift to be able to express yourself succinctly.

How To Deal With An Editor – Frustrations and Disappointments

You may feel that you are disappointed or even disheartened by the comments that come back from the editor. Read them and then put them away for a few days before you reflect upon them again.

After the initial response you will start to adjust and see the logic in the recommendations. At all times you make the final decision. A professional editor is not always right but you need to have a good reason not to accept the suggestions that are made to improve the manuscript.

Differences Between New Writers And Professional Writers

The new writer, having completed the manuscript, is glad it is finished and is keen to have it printed without editing or rewriting it. They may be so excited about what has been achieved; they find it hard to review their work objectively. The professional writer recognises the first attempt is only a draft. It needs to be rewritten several times before presenting it to a publisher.

Fine Tuning Your Final Draft

Keep revising your draft until you are satisfied that this is the best you can produce. It really doesn't matter how many times you rewrite your life story. It needs to meet a standard that you feel you can be justly proud. You reach a stage when you simply know it is now or never. Some writers are procrastinators and are fearful about allowing the completed manuscript to become a reality. People use all manner of excuses and keep saying, "It is not quite ready".

Identifying Weaknesses – Errors, Duplication, Omissions

When a writer is immersed in his story it is extremely difficult to identify weakness in the story structure. The writer knows his story in his head but it often becomes messy when transferred to words.

Muddled and confused thinking produces this messy writing. Try to clarify your thoughts before you transpose them into your writing. A writer often misses glaring errors in his work. They could be spelling or grammatical errors or weakness in the structure.

If your writing has extended over a long period there is a possibility that duplication of stories or events may appear. The writer has forgotten that the event already appears in another part of the story. Significant events could be missing from your story which could be picked up in the final editing. Some significant omissions are done purposefully in order to protect an individual. If this is the case it should be mentioned in your manuscript.

Aim For A Positive Presentation

As a writer aim to present your life story in a positive manner so that people will enjoy reading it and end up having a good feeling about it.

This is achieved by the way you present your story in describing the good and the difficult times. The tough times need not be described in a depressing manner. By describing how you have come through these times offers a sense of hope to a reader who may be struggling with similar or other difficulties.

In this final editing stage make sure that your story is not depressing but uplifting for your readers.

Checking For Accuracy

It can be an advantage to use an editor who has some knowledge of you. The final editing stage focuses on checking the accuracy of the facts presented and their consistency with the rest of your story. If your story is accurate, based on available facts, it is more likely to be believable.

Recognising Unintentional Interruptions

A good life story will flow freely and move forward from point to point.

A jarring tone or unintended interruption can occur when a new thought grabs you and you feel it should be included. At this time you look through your story and if it is essential to your story. At this final editing stage when you are reading your story aloud you may feel that this last minute thought really doesn't fit in and would be better omitted as it is an intrusion and does not add to your story.

Revise Chapter By Chapter

Do not revise your manuscript by reading it through one chapter after another. Read through one chapter and take a break for at least an hour before proceeding to the next chapter. By using this approach your mind will be fresh and alert to recognise mistakes.

Action Points To Move Your Story

There may be too much serious expression causing your story to become stiff and heavy. In the final editing stage organise your writing so it flows freely. Achieve this with the introduction of a bit of humour that breaks up the manuscript.

Now is the time to move around paragraphs to portray action. Select several action points in each chapter to give it movement. Help the reader to see where the action is in your story. Action points make an impact statement. It will help the reader to see you are not only a person of words but one also of action.

Read Your Story Aloud

Before sending your story off for the final editing read it aloud to yourself at least twice. You are more likely to pick up obvious errors when you not only see what you have written but also hear it.

On another occasion you could read it aloud to a friend to see if they can recognise ambiguities of expression.

Testing Your Story

A "Constructive Suggestion File" is worth consulting in your final effort to polish your story.

The way you create this is to give a copy of your life story to five of your friends for consideration. Ask them to make constructive suggestions for improvement in writing.

Wait until you receive the five sets of comments before you take any action. If there is a similar thought running through all the comments give it serious consideration. Make a note of other comments and decide what should be done.

Deciding On Graphics

A graphic can be a photograph or illustration which can be used to support your story. Graphics can help to break up the page and be more pleasing to the eye and this allows for the use of more white space. Graphics have to be scanned into your manuscript and will add to the cost of publication. As an author you are the one who must make a decision whether or not to use graphics.

Formatting and Assembling Your Story

Your manuscript needs to be formatted before it can appear in printed form but this work is carried out by most of the self-publishing companies. Your responsibility is to decide on the type of font and size. Assemble your story so that it follows a logical sequence. If you are going to publish your manuscript it needs to look like a book. Here is a sample guide to follow:

1. Title

2. Dedication

3. Foreword – a friend or well known personality to write introduction.

4. Table of Contents - page numbering agrees with the actual pages in your story

5. Chapter by chapter description

6.   Epilogue – life is continuing to evolve, there could be more to come.

These are only suggestions. Study other books and the way they are presented. Decide what works for you.

Proof Reading Tips

If you send your manuscript to a printer you will receive a set of proofs to correct after the final draft has been completed.

Here are a few tips:

Most printing services will supply you with a printer's guide to proof reading. Request another person to proof read, as you are likely to miss errors.

Check spelling and punctuation. Take time to check the proof against the original material.

Page numbers should be checked to make sure that there are no pages missing.

Check chapter headings and sub headings to make sure they relate to the headings.

Entries in the Table of Contents need to be identical with chapter headings and page numbers.

Do not do any rewriting of material at this time, as this will prove to be very expensive.

Sign and date your proof before returning to the printer.

Point out any imperfections – e.g. dirty marks.

Meeting A Deadline – The Ticking Clock

If the editing is to be completed by a certain date know the amount of time you need to allocate to the project. There comes a time when you feel that you need to stop editing and rewriting your material. At a subconscious level you may be procrastinating to slow down your publication date.

Moral, Ethical and Legal Dilemmas

Through your writing you will reveal your moral and ethical values. This will be clearly seen through your value clarification system and the basic belief system that you hold dear.

Moral and ethical issues are quite easily described but legal dilemmas are another issue. Say nothing you would be ashamed of, or that could be misconstrued.

Believe In Your Writing Ability

Now that you are in the final stages of editing believe you have what it takes to be a writer. I believe the "it" part can be defined as "a person who is able to stand behind his writing". You are a person who has the courage of your convictions. You know you have done you best as a writer and are ready to print your manuscript.

At this important phase of your writing you need to realise that not everyone will agree with everything you write. You may at times be called upon to explain yourself more fully or to defend the position you have taken.

It is great to have your life story published while you are still part of this planet. This can be an enriching and growth producing experience.

EXERCISES FOR LESSON TWELVE

1. Now is the time for rewriting your life story in preparation for final editing. You may do this several more times until you are absolutely sure that this is the best you can do.

2. When you reach a point of saturation and know that you can go no further then it is time to find an editor you can work with.

3. After your manuscript comes back from the editor you may feel extremely disappointed about changes that still need to be made. Believe that is the role of an editor.

4. You may even consider a rewrite at this stage. New editorial insights can present a new direction for your story. Be open at all times for editorial comment.

5. Now is the time to make any alterations before your manuscript is printed.

Self-Publishing – Your Life Story In Print

"Success comes from high hopes combined with daily discipline."

\- Zig Ziggler

Don't Let The "P" Word Scare You

P stands for publishing. Do not be scared or intimidated. Publishing is defined as "the distribution of copies ... of a work to the public". To be published, you don't have to print thousands of copies or sell them through Amazon.com.

Theoretically you could photocopy your material and then go to a printer for a special binder for one, ten, or more copies. You do not have to sell copies to be published. The publication is the finished product. If you wish to take the project further, there are more sophisticated - and more economic - ways of publishing. You decide your financial commitment to the project.

Introduction To Self-Publishing

If you would like to see your life story in print I recommend you consider self-publishing. Self-publishing is when you engage a publisher to turn your manuscript into a book. This is the most cost effective and efficient way to produce your own book, especially if there is a small print run. It means you have control of the whole process and are financially responsible. Many famous authors published their first book by this method. These include Virginia Woolf, Lord Alfred Tennyson, George Bernard Shaw and Mark Twain.

Self-publishing is an option that is becoming increasingly popular for writers of life stories. The onus is on the author to sell the books. As well as being the author of the publication he also becomes the publisher. Be careful not to be lured into long print runs because of the low unit cost. It is far better to print 50 copies at $30 than to print 500 copies at $24 and have 450 under your bed.

Printing Methods Available

The local printer – Your local printer will give you a cost for a small run. Most printers like to work from a computer disc.

Computer generated books – Books generated by a computer incur fewer overheads. Set-up costs are lower and prices can be more competitive. These can be ordered in units of twenty or thirty at a time.

Print on demand - This is perhaps the fastest growing segment of self-publishing. You pay a POD company between $1000 and $2000 to convert your manuscript into a printer–ready electronic file. This includes an application for an International Standard Book Number (ISBN) which is a ten digit number used to identify your book so that booksellers around the world can order your book using the ISBN system. The advantage of the POD system is that the book can be ready in about six weeks or less. For memoir writers it is well worth considering. It is great for small runs such as 1 – 20 or more copies. With POD you retain all your rights.

Some POD publishers give a little help with promotion but are mainly concerned with the printing of your manuscript. With this approach you do not need to produce a large number on an initial run. It is a great way to test the market. Individual copies will be dearer but you eliminate some of the risk factors.

One print run – As an author you may be satisfied with running one copy of your life story through your own printer.

How much will the book cost?

Book Sizes – the most popular book sizes are as follows:-

A4   205 x 290mm

A5   146 x 206mm

B5   176 x 250mm

Paper consideration – Your cover paper should be at least 250gsm Art Board. The inside pages should be white and on 100gsm. The spine should be made to stand out.

Colour consideration – This will add additional cost if it is in two or more colours. If you plan to sell your book this additional cost might be worthwhile.

Estimating pages – Your printer will be able to help you with this. We estimate 325 words to an A5 page (in 12 point Times font) and 550 words for B5 page.

Graphics – Think about the use of photographs. This will add additional cost to your publication.

Freight cost – Ask for the cost of the finished product delivered to your home.

Quantity – Because you are paying for the print run, keep your numbers low and realistic. It is far better to sell all the books than to have hundreds gathering dust and using valuable space.

Other costs – These could include author's correction (changes in manuscript), scanning of illustrations and proof reader if needed

Presentation ... Production ... Publication

Self-publishing involves the presentation - how the book looks. This includes cover – front and back, the spine and the way the text is set. Production includes the formatting of the book into pages, final approval of all proofs and delivery of the book to point of distribution.

Publication also involves promotion and distribution of the book and can involve sending out press releases, a book launch and arranging media interviews. If the book is for general distribution you would need a book wholesaler who takes about 40% retainer and then there is 45% or more to the retailer. The return to you is only about 10-15% of retail sales.

Australian Self Publishers

There are a number of self-publishers in Australia who are highly respected and very ethical. Some of these are listed at the end of the lesson.

You can deal with these people with confidence. Some offer a free initial consultation, others charge a fee for the initial consultation and if they are successful in receiving the order they deduct the initial quote off the contract price. Check all this out in the initial phone call.

It is wise to receive three competitive quotes in writing before deciding upon the printer. Make sure the quote includes delivery charge and GST.

Titling Your Book

It appears to be harder for non-fiction and life storywriters to find a catchy title. Fiction writers can use their imagination and creativity in a way to build intrigue, suspense and to attract reader interest. Life storywriters seem to be more limited, conservative or less imaginative in choosing a title. Consider taking the title from one of your more interesting stories in your book.

Vanity Publishers

The so-called "vanity publishers" have a tainted reputation for enticing unwitting writers with vague or misleading promises of literacy fame or fortune. Vanity publishers are found mainly overseas. Before you sign a contract, make sure that you clearly understand whom you are dealing with and what is involved. Do your homework, ask for references and look at samples, as you would do with any major expenditure.

Most vanity publishers do not edit, proofread or promote your book. If they do any of this work, it will be minimal. Booksellers are reluctant to stock books published by vanity publishers because the books are usually poorly written and unedited.

Front and Back Cover Design

Even if you are publishing your book for a limited audience spend time and thought about cover design – front and back. A good cover design can be an indication to let the reader know that you are proud about the contents of your book. Readers have a strong reaction to covers so you may wish to enlist the services of a graphic artist to make sure that the cover will stand out from the rest of the books on sale.

Pay attention to the outside back cover. This could be a synopsis of the content. It also could be a biographical outline of the author's life or a book review by two or three people respected in your community.

The Spine

The spine of your book will include the book title and name of the author. The spine needs to be strong as its main purpose is to hold the pages together.

Package Your Product

Books can live on long after we are gone. As long as the book is around your life story is there for someone to read at anytime. The size of the book does not matter but the quality does. Make sure there is a date on the book so people will know when it was first published. People sell or give away books and it can be quite surprising where the book ends up. It is your history.

Once you have published, you are bound by Law to send a copy to the National Library of Australia in Canberra and the State Library in your capital city. You may also want to send one to your local Council Library. This is another way to preserve your history, as well as adding to the local area record.

Marketing Your Book

The key to marketing is being able to use your creativity and imagination in a way that helps you to reach potential readers without spending a fortune. If you are working on a limited budget, say $1000 or less, you need to work out how to stretch your dollar.

A good press release written by a professional may take a third of your budget. If you write your own press release and have it edited by a professional your costs could be halved. Another third of your budget could be used for a book launch. You would need to rent a room, send out invitations, arrange for drinks and savouries and have a speaker to launch the book. It is estimated over 65% of people who attend a book launch buy a copy.

The rest of the money could be used to notify different target groups of your availability to speak at their functions. Have copies of the book available and refer to it in your address. Be prepared to sign copies of the book. Be available for press and radio interviews. Sell the idea to your suburban newspaper journalists who may be willing to promote it through their columns.

Be careful about spending your money on a display advertisement which could be a hit or miss approach. A letterbox drop around your area could be a worthwhile approach. I would suggest you print 5000 leaflets and look for various outlets. The saying "a fool and their money are soon parted" is so true. Spend your marketing budget wisely. Include marketing costs in deciding the retail price if you plan to sell your book.

Sell Or Give Away

Life storywriters are often confused about whether to charge for the publication or to give it away. This must always be a personal decision. I am of the opinion that anything given away is never fully valued. I believe you are entitled to recoup your publishing costs. Some copies will be given to family and close friends but other copies can perhaps be sold at cost price plus, to cover the cost of those given free.

Selling The Book On the Web

Creating a web site for yourself gets you onto a search engine and increases your market infinitely. Check on the cost of packing and posting your book within Australia and to overseas posting areas and add that to the cost. Remind overseas people to send money in Australian dollars.

Your Book Launch

Even if you only print 10 or 20 copies of your book plan a special launch. Invite your children, grandchildren and other family members and some close friends. Write a short message in the front of each book and sign it. Give a lot of thought to each inscription.

Whether you organise a picnic, dinner or barbecue make a short speech before handing out copies. Make it in some way a special occasion.

Prepare A Press Release

The opening paragraph of the press release should contain the most important facts about your story. Who, what, when, where and why. Think what is important to announce in your press release. Find an aspect that could attract media attention of local (suburban) press who might be interested in life stories. Include a copy of your profile. Try your local radio or TV stations. These people are looking for topical local stories, particularly if you live in a country town.

Writers Are Entrepreneurs

Writers create something out of nothing. They come up with an idea and run with it. Writers make a valuable contribution to our nation and can touch the lives of many people. It is a wonderful way to share your life honestly with others. A writer who enters the self-publishing field needs to have a flair for promotion to support the book in order for it to be recognised.

Word Of Mouth Publicity

Get family and friends talking about your book. It doesn't matter whether they agree with you or not. Word of mouth is the best recommendation you can get. It doesn't cost you a cent.

Technical Information

Some of this information will not apply in your situation:

Libraries: Send a copy of your book to your local, state and national libraries for their archives.

ISBN: This stands for International Standard Book Number. This will allow your book to be ordered from anywhere in the world. Your printer will help you to obtain your ISBN.

Barcode: This helps booksellers to record sales on their cash registers. Many stores add their own barcode. An organisation in Australia called EAN allocates barcode numbers. Again your printer should be able to help you.

Copyright: If you have used material which is copyright, be sure to get the author's permission before quoting from the material.

Foreword: This can be the first page of your book indicating why you have written the book.

Acknowledgement: At times a number of people may be involved – the typist, the friends who have contributed, the editor and others. All need acknowledgement for the contributions they have made.

Dedication: You may decide to dedicate this book to a very special person in your life. Be sure to obtain their permission.

Disclaimer: This indicates you have proceeded with care and diligence and every effort has been made to make sure all facts are correct as presented.

Buyers And Readers

In its lifetime your book could pass through many hands. It could be sold to a second hand book dealer who then resells it. It could be sold at a garage sale. You never know where your book will end up. People borrow a book from a friend or get a copy from a public library.

The Browsers

You may know exactly whom I am talking about. You could be a browser. It is a person who has time to spare whilst shopping or waiting for an appointment who enters a bookstore to kill time. It is a recognised fact that more women buy books than men.

A browser is attracted by the title of the book, comments on the back page and the first five paragraphs of the book. This is the reason why the first page should raise curiosity level to encourage the reader to continue on.

Reflecting On Your Finished Book

After your book has been published take time to reflect upon your many experiences. Give yourself a pat on the back for a job well done. May your story live forever.

Take time to relive some of these experiences. In writing your life story you have left behind a rich legacy. Perhaps it may not be fully appreciated now but in the years to come with age and maturity you could be remembered with fondness and love.

If your life story has inspired another person to write his story then it has been doubly successful.

List Of Self-Publishers

COMPANY	ADDRESS	CONTACT
Breakout Design + Print	65 Bellevue St Glebe 2037	(02) 9660 9111
Jennings Publishing	PO Box 3569 North Mackay 4720	1800 111 084
Hippo Books	18 Primrose Ave Rosebery 2018	(02) 9313 7811
Fast Books	16 Darghan St Glebe 2037	(02) 9692 0166
Seaview Press	186 Seaview Rd Henley Beach 5022	(08) 8235 1535
Mini Publishing	41 Cecil St Gordon 2072	1800 108 808
Garr Publishing	464 The Entrance Rd Erina Heights 2260	(02) 4367 7223
The Oracle Press	1 Burke Court Mt Ommaney 4074	(07) 3279 3831
D Books	146 Arthur St North Sydney 2060	(02) 9954 5205
Ligare Pty Ltd	138 Bond Rd Riverwood 2210	(02) 9533 2655
Temple House Pty Ltd	PO Box 1042 Hartwell Vic	
Hender Publishing	112 Haydon St Murrurundi 2338	(02) 6546 6632
R.S. Publishing	PO Box 722 Newcastle 2300	www.rspublishing.com.au
Zeus Publications	PO Box 2554 Burleigh MDC 4220	(07) 5575 5141

For information only – no responsibility accepted

EXERCISES FOR LESSON THIRTEEN

1. Write a Foreword to your book describing the reasons why you have made this effort.

2. Investigate the best and most economical way to publish your book.

3. Obtain three quotes in writing. The lowest quote may not always be the best.

4. Think about the realistic number of copies you can dispose of and form of distribution. Consider a function to launch your life story.

5. Reward yourself in some way for your accomplishment. Be kind to yourself.

Also Available from the Author

Life Is For Living – Graham Ascough's Autobiography

Graham Ascough writes with humour, sensitivity and clarity and shares his "Philosophy For The 21st Century". He blends psychological insights and spiritual truths. You will enter the world of advertising, marketing and journalism. Then share the story of ministry, counselling and as an operator of a bed and breakfast. Finally he will reveal his thoughts and dreams as a writer.

Oh Happy, Happy Days! – The New Rules of Retirement

A priceless gift for those who are about to retire ... an absolute must-have for singles and couples already retired.

> *"Graham Ascough has been a top quality counsellor for several decades. His vast experience of life comes to the fore in this book, and you profit from it."*
> – Everald Compton AM

Over 1550 proven concepts show you how to re-focus the young person within and shape your retirement as the best years of your life!

OH HAPPY, HAPPY DAYS!

The new rules of retirement

Live it, really, really live it!

GRAHAM L ASCOUGH

To purchase books or to contact Graham Ascough:

Phone: (02) 9879 6582
Fax: (02) 9879 7439
Mobile: 0413 363 947
Web: www.grahamascough.com